D0970877

## CONTEMPORARY WRITERS

General Editors
MALCOLM BRADBURY
and
CHRISTOPHER BIGSBY

## DORIS LESSING

# DORIS
# LESSING

## LORNA SAGE

METHUEN
LONDON AND NEW YORK

First published in 1983 by
Methuen & Co. Ltd
11 New Fetter Lane, London EC4P 4EE
Published in the USA by
Methuen & Co.
in association with Methuen, Inc.
733 Third Avenue, New York, NY 10017

Typeset by Rowland Phototypesetting Ltd
Printed in Great Britain by
Richard Clay (The Chaucer Press) Ltd
Bungay, Suffolk

British Library Cataloguing in Publication Data

Sage, Lorna
Doris Lessing. – (Contemporary writers)
1. Lessing, Doris – criticism and interpretation
I. Title     II. Series
823'.914     PR6023.E8332/
ISBN 0-416-31730-8

Library of Congress Cataloging in Publication Data

Sage, Lorna.
Doris Lessing.
(Contemporary writers)
Bibliography: p.
1. Lessing, Doris May, 1919–      – Criticism and
interpretation. I. Title.  II. Series.
PR6023.E833Z878 1983     823'.914     82-20846
ISBN 0-416-31730-8 (pbk.)

# CONTENTS

# GENERAL EDITORS' PREFACE

Over the past twenty years or so, it has become clear that a decisive change has taken place in the spirit and character of contemporary writing. There now exists around us, in fiction, drama and poetry, a major achievement which belongs to our experience, our doubts and uncertainties, our ways of perceiving – an achievement stylistically radical and novel, and likely to be regarded as quite as exciting, important and innovative as that of any previous period. This is a consciousness and a confidence that has grown very slowly. In the 1950s it seemed that, somewhere amidst the dark realities of the Second World War, the great modernist impulse of the early years of this century had exhausted itself, and that the post-war arts would be arts of recessiveness, pale imitation, relative sterility. Some, indeed, doubted the ability of literature to survive the experiences of holocaust. A few major figures seemed to exist, but not a style or a direction. By the 1960s the confidence was greater, the sense of an avant-garde returned, the talents multiplied, and there was a growing hunger to define the appropriate styles, tendencies and forms of a new time. And by the 1970s it was not hard to see that we were now surrounded by a remark-able, plural, innovative generation, indeed several layers of generations, whose works represented a radical inquiry into contemporary forms and required us to read and under-stand – or, often, to read and *not* understand – in quite new ways. Today, as the 1980s start, that cumulative post-war achievement has acquired a degree of coherence that allows for critical response and understanding; hence the present series.

We thus start it in the conviction that the age of Beckett, Borges, Nabokov, Bellow, Pynchon, Robbe-Grillet, Golding, Murdoch, Fowles, Grass, Handke and Calvino, of Albee, Mamet, Shepard, Ionesco, Orton, Pinter and Stoppard, of Ginsberg, Lowell, Ashbery, Paz, Larkin and Hughes, and many another, is indeed an outstanding age of international creation, striking experiment, and some degree of aesthetic coherence. It is a time that has been described as 'post-modern', in the sense that it is an era consequent to modernism yet different from it, having its own distinctive preoccupations and stylistic choices. That term has its limitations, because it is apt to generate too precise definitions of the contemporary experiment, and has acquired rather too specific associations with contemporary American writing; but it does help concentrate our sense of living in a distinctive period. With the new writing has come a new criticism or rather a new critical theorem, its thrust being 'structuralist' or 'deconstructive' – a theorem that not only coexists with but has affected that writing (to the point where many of the best theorists write fictions, the best fictionalists write criticism). Again, its theory can be hermetic and enclosing, if not profoundly apocalyptic; but it points to the presence in our time of a new sense of the status of word and text, author and reader, which shapes and structures the making of modern form.

The aim of 'Contemporary Writers' is to consider some of the most important figures in this scene, looking from the standpoint of and at the achievement of the writers themselves. Its aims are eclectic, and it will follow no tight definition of the contemporary; it will function on the assumption that contemporary writing is by its nature multidirectional and elusive, since styles and directions keep constantly changing in writers who, unlike the writers of the past, are continuous, incomplete, not dead (though several of these studies will address the careers of those who, though dead, remain our contemporaries, as many of those who continue to write are manifestly not). A fair criticism of living writers must be assertive but also provisional, just as a fair sense of contemporary style must be open to that most crucial of contemporary awarenesses, that of the suddenness of change. We do not assume, then, that there is one right path to contemporary experiment, nor that a self-conscious reflexiveness, a deconstructive strategy, an art of performance or a metafictional mode is the only one of current importance. As Iris Murdoch said, 'a strong agile realism which is of course not photographic naturalism' – associated perhaps especially with British writing, but also with Latin-American and American – is also a major component of modern style.

So in this series we wish to identify major writers, some of whom are avant-garde, others who are familiar, even popular, but all of whom are in some serious sense contemporary and in some contemporary sense serious. The aim is to offer brief, lucid studies of their work which draw on modern theoretical issues but respond, as much modern criticism does not, to their distinctiveness and individual interest. We have looked for contributors who are engaged with their subjects – some of them being significant practising authors themselves, writing out of creative experience, others of whom are critics whose interest is personal as well as theoretical. Each volume will provide a thorough account of the author's work so far, a solid bibliography, a personal judgement – and, we hope, an enlarged understanding of writers who are important, not only because of the individual force of their work, but because they are ours in ways no past writer could really be.

*Norwich, England*                               MALCOLM BRADBURY
                                                  CHRISTOPHER BIGSBY

# PREFACE AND ACKNOWLEDGEMENTS

Doris Lessing is a writer of epic scale and scope. One of the heavy mob, somebody once said – one of those figures (the chronicler, the prophet) who awaken our rather shamefaced desire to have our culture interpreted for us, while at the same time arousing all our scepticism about the possibility of its being done; a writer who has involved herself in a wide world of issues, from colonial oppression in southern Africa, where she grew up, to the recurrent threat of nuclear war. An important writer, as we say, though 'important' is always a double-edged epithet, since we are very ready to suspect our oracles of artistic bad faith. Lessing lives and breathes in the dangerous atmosphere of watchwords, catchphrases, labels. Our society, she wrote in *The Four-Gated City* (1969), is like 'one of those sea creatures who have tentacles or arms equipped with numbing poisons':

> anything new, whether hostile or helpful, must be stunned into immobility. . . . The process is accomplished, in this society, through words. . . . communism, traitor, espionage, homosexuality, teenage violence. . . . Or anger, or commitment, or satire. . . . Anarchy, irresponsibility, decadence, selfishness – into this box, behind this label, gets put every kind of behaviour by which the creature is made nervous. . . . quick, quick, a new word, a new label, 'commitment', perhaps? 'mysticism?' (*FGC*, pp. 465–6)

9

This, for her, is the writer's proper battleground, the public arena where meanings are routinely overrun and vandalized. She is a utopian. She wants to regroup and mobilize the imaginative forces we dissipate in this cold war.

Militant metaphors are appropriate. She is not – despite the title of her essay on the art of the novel, 'The Small Personal Voice' (1957) – a private or self-contained writer. She belongs in a tradition stemming from what Ellen Moers (in *Literary Women*) called the 'epic age' of women's writing: the period in the nineteenth century when women novelists wrote gallantly and crusadingly about poverty, slavery, class conflict – about everything, it sometimes seems, except the 'woman question'. And, though Doris Lessing is almost as famous for being a woman as for being 'important', this is rather her position too. Like Christina Stead (a writer of a slightly earlier generation, but then Lessing was brought up in an old-fashioned colonial society, and got her higher education in the Communist Party), she thought feminism at once obvious – part of the radical package – and somehow self-pitying. As a result, the success of *The Golden Notebook* in the 1960s as a portent of a new era of feminist consciousness seemed to her anomalous. She had meant, in that novel, to orchestrate a whole series of break-downs: a crisis in radical politics (her heroine Anna Wulf leaves the Communist Party, as Lessing had done in 1956); a parallel disillusion with psychoanalytic truisms (Anna leaves her analyst, and falls apart her own way); a destructive, vagrant, post-marital phase in relations between the sexes; and the disease of public language that eats into Anna's vocation as a writer. Sexual politics was only one aspect of her theme; and, moreover, her men were as damaged as her women by the outworn roles they played.

On the longer view, however, she and her 'sex-war' readers are not wildly at odds. She may write in a magisterial manner, but she speaks for undergrounds and subcultures, and is honour-bound to collude with unsettling, centrifugal forces. In this sense her fiction feeds into the newest women's writing, as it fed off the old. Her career to date displays an exemplary transformation from a socialist realism that recalls her nineteenth-century predecessors, to the speculative forms she borrows from 'mystical' writing and space fiction which mark her kinship with (for example) Margaret Atwood in Canada, or Joyce Carol Oates in America. The chronicler is no longer a realist – reality is too fractured and crazy for that. Yet she retains her epic ambitions, and so has it both ways – not 'just' a woman, but a sibyl, a wise woman, a mutant matriarch.

She is, after all, an expert in unsettlement. The colonial experience – the colonial metaphor – is central to her identity as a writer. Her earliest African writing and her most recent space fiction alike are preoccupied with the transience of our world-pictures – with ways, that is, of analysing and heightening their transience, of decentring imaginative life. So long as we behave imaginatively like colonists (for her the archetypal enemies of change), we are doomed to repeat ourselves wherever we turn – doomed to cast ourselves in dubious character-parts, and to impose dead patterns on the worlds we inhabit. Her writing sets out to erase some of the most stubborn boundaries on our mental maps. Other writers make us stand to attention when they say 'I'. With her the collective 'we' is what does it, and she calls up the nightmares old and new that shadow that particular pronoun. Who are 'we'? Her fiction, asking the question, cuts to the centre of contemporary cultural paranoia, and challenges us to imagine a shareable space.

The author and publisher would like to thank the following for permission to reproduce copyright material: Michael Joseph Ltd and Simon & Schuster, Inc. for extracts from *The Golden Notebook*; Granada Publishing Ltd and Simon & Schuster, Inc. for extracts from *Martha Quest*; Granada Publishing Ltd and Alfred A. Knopf, Inc. for extracts from *The Four-Gated City*.

*Norwich, England, 1982*                          LORNA SAGE

# A NOTE ON THE TEXTS

Page references to quotations from Doris Lessing's fiction are taken from the editions listed below. The following abbreviations have been used:

GH    *Going Home* (London: Michael Joseph, 1957)
CAS   *Collected African Stories*, vols 1 and 2 (St Albans: Panther, 1979)
GS    *The Grass is Singing* (London: Michael Joseph, 1950)
MQ    *Martha Quest* (St Albans: Panther, 1966)
PM    *A Proper Marriage* (St Albans: Panther, 1966)
RS    *A Ripple from the Storm* (St Albans: Panther, 1966)
IPE   *In Pursuit of the English* (St Albans: Panther, 1980)
CS    *Collected Stories*, vols 1 and 2 (St Albans: Triad/Panther, 1979)
RI    *Retreat to Innocence* (London: Sphere, 1967)
GN    *The Golden Notebook* (Harmondsworth: Penguin, 1964)
L     *Landlocked* (St Albans: Panther, 1967)
FGC   *The Four-Gated City* (St Albans: Panther, 1972)
BDH   *Briefing for a Descent into Hell* (St Albans: Panther, 1972)
SBD   *The Summer Before the Dark* (Harmondsworth: Penguin, 1975)
MS    *The Memoirs of a Survivor* (London: Octagon Press, 1974)

S *Shikasta* (London: Cape, 1979)

MBZ *The Marriages Between Zones Three, Four, and Five* (London: Cape, 1980)

SE *The Sirian Experiments* (London: Cape, 1981)

MRP *The Making of the Representative for Planet 8* (London: Cape, 1982)

# 1

## AFRICA

Doris Lessing was born in 1919 in 'Persia' (now Iran) and grew up and lived in 'Southern Rhodesia' (now Zimbabwe) until 1949, when she came to London. Or, rather, 'London': since for her being a colonial has meant that names, places, the colourings of the map have always had something provisional – something arbitrary and ominous – about them. The British colonial society in which she developed her distinctive vision, and where her first novels and stories are set, was marginal and embattled and gruesomely suburban. As she wrote, sardonically, looking back:

> Not long ago people set foot for the colonies – the right sort of people, that is, in a spirit of risking everything and damning the cost. These days, a reverse immigration is in progress. The horizon conquerors now set sail or take wing for England, which in this sense means London, determined to conquer it, but on their own terms. (*IPE*, p. 13)

However, the London she eventually arrived and settled in seemed to her hardly less precarious than the society she had left. Her world is one of violence and change. 'All the stories here are set in a society which is more short-lived than most,' she wrote in the 1972 Preface to Volume 1 of her *Collected African Stories*: 'white-dominated Africa cannot last very long. But looking around the world now, there isn't a way of living anywhere that doesn't change and dissolve like clouds as you watch.' She too has changed a great deal since her first novel

15

*The Grass is Singing* came out in 1950, but the colonial situation has left its mark on all her writing. Her very openness to change seems, paradoxically enough, to spring from her experience of the entrenched mythologies of white domination.

A 1956 piece she wrote for the *New Statesman* ('Being Prohibited') contains an anecdote that nicely measures degrees of displacement. She is recalling the first time she crossed the border between Southern Rhodesia and South Africa, when she was 16:

> I was not, as one says, politically conscious; nor did I know the score. I knew no more, in fact, than on which side my bread was buttered. But I already felt uneasy about being a member of the Herrenvolk. When the immigration official reached me, I had written on the form: *Nationality*, British, *Race*, European; and it was the first time in my life I had had to claim myself as a member of one race and disown the others. . . .
>
> The immigration man . . . looked suspiciously at my form for a long time before saying that I was in the wrong part of the train. I did not understand him. (I forgot to mention that where the form asked, Where were you born?, I had written, Persia.)
>
> 'Asiatics', said he, 'have to go to the back of the train. . . .'
>
> 'But', I said, 'I am not an Asiatic.'
>
> The compartment had five other females in it; skirts were visibly being drawn aside. To prove my bona fides I should, of course, have exclaimed with outraged indignation at any such idea.[1]

This time she was allowed in; in 1956, when she revisited Southern Rhodesia and once more attempted the South African border, she was not, and on her return to London found she was banned from Southern Rhodesia too.

She toys, in the *New Statesman* piece, with the irritating suspicion that perhaps, after all, it was her Persian birth rather than her 'red' anti-racist politics that made her a prohibited

16

alien. Race is compounded of hallucinations and fictions (including one's own); later in London a rejected landlady, hearing that Lessing comes from Africa, mutters darkly, 'I've known people before, calling it sunburn' (*IPE*, p. 41). The major irony in all this, though – as her book on the 1956 African visit, *Going Home* (1957), makes clear – is that the bureaucratic ban, whatever its motive, merely confirmed her own self-banishment. Africa itself, as opposed to its colonial regimes, was for her a vital source of imaginative food – 'This was my air, my landscape, and above all, my sun' – but 'Africa belongs to the Africans; the sooner they take it back the better' (*GH*, p. 12). Reviewing other (white) African writers, she has always recognized the same nostalgic taste in the head, and always jealously denied them what she denies herself – belonging, possession. Thus Karen Blixen ('Isak Dinesen', whose *Out of Africa* first came out in 1938) strikes Lessing as almost ludicrously 'feudal' in not being able to see that, for all her ecstasy among 'rivers, hills, plains, creatures', 'her 6000 acres were not hers'. Laurens Van Der Post's travel books, excitedly penetrating the dark continent, provoked yet a meaner rebuff: 'The African landscape is still, thank God, impersonal and indifferent to man'.[2]

Africa struck Europeans as, simply, space. Lessing recalls from her childhood a passing wanderer, an old prospector, shouting angrily: 'Man needs an empty space somewhere for his spirit to rest in' (*GH*, p. 13). Such figures retain an equivocal innocence – they wander into her fiction too, and when they do it is with a background sense that fiction is where they belong. One of her latest and best African stories, 'The Story of a Non-Marrying Man', first published in a 1972 collection, glimpses such a character in Johnny Blakeworthy, who alternates tragicomically between domestic space and 'going native' in the wild landscape. Johnny's dubious trail of bigamous marriages (is the missing husband always the same man?) leads from one town/job/set of china and cushions and curtains to another; we track him through gossip, a magazine story, recollections of recollections:

Then he drifted North, out of the white man's towns, and up into those parts that had not been 'opened up to white settlement', and where the Africans were still living, though not for long, in their traditional ways. And there at last he found a life that suited him, and a woman with whom he lived in kindness. (*CAS* 2, pp. 43–4)

The cadence of 'settling', coming at last to rest, is a deeply ironic one – not least because it is precisely the presence of Johnny's shadow half (the settler) that has already largely destroyed the 'traditional ways' that seem so spacious.

Settling is, for Lessing, displacement mystified and disguised. Her most 'African' stories (those that encounter the empty landscape most directly) are about coming to a dead halt. The two stories she placed first in Volume 1 of *Collected African Stories* perhaps act this out most clearly. 'The Old Chief Mshlanga' traces a white child's 'naturalization' in Africa. To begin with, she sees the landscape through the images of English fairy tales; only gradually does it become familiar, hers, and then she arrogantly possesses it. Her right seems, indeed, guaranteed (and her arrogance diminished) when she encounters the old chief, the first African she learns to respect:

> it was as if I stood aside to watch a slow intimate dance of landscape and men, a very old dance, whose steps I could not learn.
>
> But I thought: this is my heritage, too; I was bred here; it is my country as well as the black man's country; and there is plenty of room for all of us . . . (*CAS* 1, p. 17)

The narrative has moved by now to the first person, as if to underline the self-knowledge its heroine is growing into, but actually to prepare for a very opposite end. Ego accepts no bounds: the girl searches out the unsettled land where Chief Mshlanga still rules, and finds herself first lost and seized with panic, and then, when she reaches his village, baffled in the face not of emptiness but of another society where nothing about herself is welcome. Nothing happens, or can, except that as she

18

walks home 'there was now a queer hostility in the landscape
. . . as strong as a wall, as intangible as smoke' (*CAS* 1, p. 22);
and that, before long, the chief and his kraal are moved to 'a
proper native reserve'.

Like 'The Old Chief Mshlanga', the second story, 'Sunrise on
the Veld', is an anti-fable that traces a blocking of romanticism,
a shrinkage of space. The adolescent boy protagonist leaps and
yells his way through the dawning landscape to confront a
scene that seems to come from 'a dream': 'a strange beast that
was horned and drunken-legged. . . . that had black ragged
tufts of fur . . . with patches of raw flesh beneath (*CAS* 1, p. 29),
which he recognizes with sickening slowness as a buck being
eaten alive by ants. His euphoria drains into another feeling –
stoicism: 'this is what happens, this is how things work. . . . the
ants must eat too' (*CAS* 1, pp. 30–1). But this also is too
spacious, too distant a perspective, and, as the heat of full
daylight grows uncomfortable and the buck's white skeleton is
picked clean and visible, he shrinks into himself. The buck's
leg, he sees, was broken somehow: the thought that the same
fate might have befallen him is so obvious and terrible that he
can't think it. He thinks instead of the bucks he has 'missed'
with a careless shot, and plods wearily home through a maze of
responsibilities.

There isn't 'room for all of us'. The landscape is almost
claustrophobically crowded: one is neither free nor fated in it,
but meshed in complexity. And yet the myths are so simple.
Lessing, looking for analogies, finds 'European' colonial myths
'American' (another displacement):

> They are of the frontiersman and the lone-wolf; the brave
> white woman house-making in primitive conditions; the
> child who gets himself an education and so a status beyond
> his parents. . . . Yet these images have no longer anything to
> do with what is going on now in Central Africa. (*GH*, p. 58)

Her accounts of her own family stress the sheer unreality in
which they lived. The fullest is 'My Father', and the story it tells
is one she had already touched on many times in her fiction.

Her father, crippled in the First World War, had married her mother (his nurse) in 1919. He 'could not face being a bank clerk in England ... after the trenches ... went off to the Imperial Bank of Persia', but was still 'longing for something freer, because as a bank official he could not let go into the dream-logged personality that was awaiting him.' On leave in 1925 in London, he visited an empire exhibition, and 'on an impulse' emigrated to farm in Southern Rhodesia:

> Soon, there was my father in a cigar-shaped house of thatch and mud on the top of a kopje. . . . a couple of hundred miles south from the Zambesi, a hundred or so west from Mozambique. . . . Logamundi – gold country, tobacco country, maize country – wild, almost empty. (The Africans had been turned off it into reserves.) Our neighbours were four, five, seven miles off. In front of the house . . . no neighbours, nothing . . .

Her mother

> After a period of neurotic illness ... became brave and resourceful. But she never saw that her husband was not living in a real world. . . . We were always about to 'get off the farm'. A miracle would do it – a sweepstake, a gold-mine, a legacy.

Her father's dreams, over the years, grew wilder: 'It could be gold divining. . . . It could be the relation between the minerals of the earth and of the moon.'[3]

The long story 'Eldorado' links this special brand of madness with the figure of the old prospector, 'an old weather-stained man' whose life story, like one 'from a child's adventure book in its simplicities of luck and bad fortune' (*CAS* 1, p. 296), fires an unsuccessful farmer, Alec Barnes, with the glamour of the search for gold. Little by little, the 'settler' Alec is transformed into a crazy wanderer, zigzagging across his farmland 'divining' gold with a rod. His new vision of 'the reefs and shales and silts and rivers of the underworld' (*CAS* 1, p. 300) is full of vivid details but fatally askew – as, we realize, his picture of the farm has always been. Clearing new bush every year, and eroding the soil, was just as crazy, if more discreetly so. His whole relation to the landscape is vitiated by his dreams of freedom and space:

> He used to stand at the edge of a field, gazing dimly across it at a ridge of bush which rose sharp to the great blue sky. . . . He would stand on a moonlight night staring across the fields which now appeared like a diffusing green sea. . . . Distance – that was what he needed. It was what he had left England to find. (*CAS* 1, p. 291)

When his son Paul, goaded into practicality, finds gold on the farm without the least aid from his divinations, Alec's madness comes full circle and closes round him. And yet, we're meant to feel, Paul is old and weary before his time, impoverished by not being able to believe in the 'childish' adventure story, knowing himself an alien, and responsible.

Lessing often treats the fruitless yearning for space as a peculiarly English neurosis. Stories like 'The Second Hut' and 'The De Wets Come to Kloof Grange' contrast the English in Africa with 'poor white' Afrikaners, who are portrayed as indeed almost African, inhabiting the space, their Dutch ancestry bred out. In *Going Home* the Afrikaner is 'the original; something new; something that cannot be seen in any other continent. . . . as indigenous as the Africans' (*GH*, p. 20), and thus set on a tragic collision course. The English, however, remain unrooted: 'My parents were English because they yearned for England, but knew they could never live in it again because of its conservatism, narrowness and tradition' (*IPE*, p. 12). The colony – its British part at least – is populated by refugees from history who, having mislaid 'their' England, are fatally adrift, even while they appropriate the land, and become more and more determined on a 'white' Rhodesia.

*

We begin, then, from displacement, from an inability to accept the frontier myths. The closest Lessing comes to spelling out the effect of a colonial family background in the making of a writer is not in any of the personal interviews but in her 1968

21

Afterword to Olive Schreiner's novel *The Story of an African Farm* (1885):

> To the creation of a woman novelist seem to go certain psychological ingredients; at least, often enough to make it interesting. One of them, a balance between father and mother where the practicality, the ordinary sense, cleverness, and worldly ambition is on the side of the mother; and the father's life is so weighted with dreams and ideas and imaginings that their joint life gets lost in what looks like a hopeless muddle and failure, but which holds a potentiality for something that must be recognized as better, on a different level, than what ordinary sense or cleverness can achieve.[4]

This Schreiner family scenario is recognizably also that of Lessing's autobiographical pieces, and of much of her African fiction, and it belongs not only to psychology but to (colonial) psycho-history. When the old male adventure story turns to 'dream' (leaving women to cope, as in so many of her stories, with daily living and planning), a new and problematic imaginative horizon opens up for a daughter. The very failure of 'settlement', for her, may be a clue to rewriting her world, transcending 'ordinary sense'.

Certainly, Lessing's rejection or perversion of her part in the scenario ('the child who gets himself an education and so a status beyond his parents') did make her encounters with other people's books particularly intense and personal and, in a sense, egalitarian:

> What did I read? The best – the classics of European and American literature. One of the advantages of not being educated was that I didn't have to waste time on the second-best. . . .
>
> I could have been educated – formally, that is – but I felt some neurotic rebellion against my parents who wanted me to be brilliant academically. I simply contracted out of the whole thing and educated myself.[5]

She left school at 14 (a boy as bright would hardly have been allowed to) and took more than ten years to make her vocation real. Biography here is (very deliberately, on her part) sketchy: she worked intermittently in the capital Salisbury (as nurse-maid, telephone operator), married a civil servant there on the eve of the war, when she was 19, and had two children. In 1942 the marriage broke up, and she joined a communist group founded by British servicemen and other temporary exiles in the colony; she was divorced in 1943, and in 1945 married a German communist, Gottfried Lessing. In 1949 she was again divorced, and came to London with the small son of her second marriage, and the manuscript of her first novel:

> Let's put it this way: I do not think that marriage is one of my talents. . . .
>
> I wrote some bad novels in my teens. I always knew I would be a writer, but not until I was quite old – twenty-six or -seven – did I realize that I'd better stop saying I was *going* to be one and get down to business. I was working in a lawyer's office at the time, and I remember walking in and saying to my boss, 'I'm giving up my job because I'm going to write a novel.' He very properly laughed, and I indignantly walked home and wrote *The Grass is Singing* . . .[6]

The communist group seems to have provided a rehearsal for exile, and at the same time a framework for reading – and rewriting – the colony's myths. C. J. Driver, in a 1974 'Profile' of Lessing, comments: 'In a sense the Communists in Rhodesia during the war were her university teachers.'[7] Obviously, though, the curriculum was a distinctive one. And here, as in her earlier voracious reading, Lessing encountered books and ideas with an autodidact's directness, unmediated by a national culture. She herself later talked of the group as spectacularly rootless:

> It must have been blessed by Lenin from his grave, it was so pure. . . . if we had been in any other part of the world, where in fact there was a Communist party, the beautiful purity of the ideas we were trying to operate couldn't have worked.[8]

None the less at the time its unashamedly intellectual and analytic idiom gave her a kind of context, and shaped the writer she saw herself to be: a demystifier, a critical observer of social processes and systems, an outsider who could see through to the inside, a radical realist. Lessing's initial creative roots lie in this critical, political culture, and what in turn lay behind that: a notion of the novel as a radical political form, fed by social facts and social urgencies. And this was Doris Lessing's primary starting place as a writer, a place she was later to transform and alter through the long search of the novels that followed.

*

Social realism was, in fact, a popular mode in the London she came to in 1949, as British writers began to occupy the new landscape of the welfare state. Lessing's note was thus not entirely independent of the contemporary direction of fiction, but a related yet oblique expression of it. Her stories reflected her political background and her sense of the claims of realism; they insisted on the crowdedness and social complexity of the apparent mythic emptiness of Africa, portrayed the white settlers as adrift from the processes of history. *The Grass is Singing*, her first novel, is yet another pursuit of the 'true' story underlying colonial fictions, but this time more systematic and complete. It is a crammed and urgent book, impatient to get down in 'black and white' (a phrase that reverberates with irony) all that is unspoken – and so, in a sense, made white, whitewashed – in settler society. The opening chapter shows the white-out at work, framing the narrative with its 'Murder Mystery' newspaper clipping – 'Mary Turner, wife of Richard Turner, a farmer at Ngesi . . . found murdered. . . . houseboy . . . confessed. . . . No motive. . . . in search of valuables' – and Tony Marston, the Turners' manager, fresh from England, is expertly thwarted when he suggests to the neighbour Charlie Slatter and the police sergeant that there was a motive, or at least a logic, in the murder. The local whites close ranks by some 'sixth sense', in 'silent, unconscious agreement': 'Everyone behaved like a flock of birds who communicate – or so it seems – by means of a kind of telepathy' (*GS*, p. 10). Tony's sense that 'the important thing . . . was to understand the background, the circumstances, the characters of Dick and Mary, the pattern of their lives' (*GS*, p. 26) remains unspoken. He mentally rehearses an alternative scene in which he protests that 'Either the white people are responsible for their behaviour, or they are not. It takes two to make a murder – a murder of this kind' (*GS*, p. 32). He has already been swamped by the 'unrealized', 'unacknowledged', 'instinctive' (*GS*, pp. 27–8) determination of Slatter and the sergeant that the 'Mystery' must not be investigated. The inside story that follows is not Tony's – he is dismissed to wander into an office job, and learn silence – but belongs to an anonymous 'One' ('If one was looking for a symbol'; *GS*, p. 36) who is armed against the colony's mysteries, and determined that the pattern of the Turners' lives shall be realized, acknowledged, brought to consciousness.

Dick and Mary Turner are familiar Lessing characters: he the dreaming, hopeless farmer, impotently in love with the land; she practical and energetic but (as a long flashback reveals) emotionally blocked by her parents' poverty and misery, and her mother's contempt for her father. Here, though – as in none of the stories – their marriage precipitates a mutual disintegration that 'lets in' the bush and the natives, and the past history that both of them – but especially Mary – must repress in order to survive. As must the white colony. Another 'African' writer, Dan Jacobson, in another context, explains why:

> A colonial culture is one which has no memory. . . . Precisely because the sense of history is so deficient, [historical] enmities tend to be regarded as so many given, unalterable facts of life. . . . A white South African, for example, feels no need to ask himself how the black man came to be his inferior; he simply knows that the black man *is* inferior.[9]

Lessing's characters enter on a gradual nightmare in which

they lose touch with the present-tense certainties of the language of whiteness. They 'go native' – not in the romantic way early adventurers managed, or dreamed, but amid squalor and confusion.

Mary is at the centre of the process, trapped on the farm into re-enacting the failure of her parents' marriage, venting on the Africans the fury she feels at Dick's dreamy shiftlessness, until she rouses in herself the long-repressed guilt and fear of her childhood. Stunned into consciousness, she realizes, at a rare still point that forms the pivot of the novel, that she and Dick are all wrong, and cannot change:

> That short time, she looked at everything straight, without illusions, seeing herself and Dick and their relationship to each other and to the farm, and their future, without a shadow of false hope, as honest and stark as the truth itself. And she knew she could not bear this sad clear-sightedness for long; that, too, was part of the truth. (*GS*, p. 168)

There is no future, only the past, and the past returns in the person of Moses, a native who becomes her houseboy and her incubus, and whose face bears the scar of her whip. That signature of her violence causes an intimacy between them which, in her despair, she cannot counter; he builds on it what seems to her a secret dialogue of domination. In her mind one taboo blurs into another: 'her feeling was one of a strong and irrational fear, a deep uneasiness, and even – though this she did not know, would have died rather than acknowledge – of some dark attraction' (*GS*, p. 190). Moses becomes the bizarre custodian of her fantasies of hatred and yearning towards her despised father. And she does indeed die rather than acknowledge it: faced with Charlie Slatter's disgust at what he suspects of her condition, and the new manager Tony Marston's chivalrous pity, she rejects Moses, and he kills her. Dick, lost in his separate fantasy of 'his' land, is mad, 'wandering in and out of the bush with his hands full of leaves and earth' (*GS*, p. 13).

Whether Mary has consummated her 'dark attraction', and what is the meaning of Moses's indifference, almost paralysis, after 'the satisfaction of his completed revenge' (*GS*, p. 256), we don't know with any certainty; and this mystery has reminded readers of the enigma of Conrad's *Heart of Darkness*. However, the resemblance seems misleading, especially since it gives Lessing's novel a 'spatial', static symbolism it fights against, as do the stories (compare the rejected perspective – '*It was right and nothing could alter it*' – in 'A Sunrise on the Veld'). Lessing's 'darkness' is less romantic, much more to do with the repressive mechanisms of society and psyche. Thus it is when Mary recognizes her (despised, denied, phallic) father in Moses – 'They advanced together, one person, and she could smell, not the native smell, but the unwashed smell of her father' (*GS*, p. 203) – that the real breaking of taboos happens. Putting it this way, of course, suggests another connection, with Lawrence, who is indeed the writer she is closest to here. The Turners' marriage, and Mary's parents' marriage, seem thoroughly Lawrentian (maimed man/'phallic', disappointed woman), as does the implication that this is a hidden disease of the whole culture. However, one echo – Mary watching Moses bathe, as Connie Chatterly watched Mellors – serves, deliberately or not, to emphasize the difference between class barriers and race barriers. Mellors's skin was startlingly white.

Lessing's way of appropriating what she wants from the writers of an earlier generation has sometimes worked in reverse, so that her concerns become subsumed in theirs.[10] For that reason, it seems worth somewhat labouring the point that *The Grass is Singing* is about a historical and psychological stalemate: repression meshed with oppression. Settlers' imaginations and memories have to be wiped clean – as Charlie Slatter and the sergeant wipe Mary's case out of history – because, if there is a 'dark' past, then there is a black future. But does Moses represent that? Lessing is self-trapped here. To explain Moses, to write him out, might well be to *white* him out, even if one did it very differently from the newspaper clipping's stereotype of the thieving houseboy. But then again, to leave him blank, in a book so conscious of the oppressive

27

function of silence, is deeply embarrassing. What this dilemma reveals is a vital problem in Lessing's writing. How much can one represent? How much, that is, can one find others in oneself, in experience, imagination and language? In short, though on a different level, Lessing the writer is encountering her settlers' problem, and hasn't found a solution. Yes, obviously, Moses 'is' the future, though he'll be briskly tried and hanged, and though the Charlie Slatters will become more efficient at denying history – and though Lessing leaves him unfathomable. But his action remains empty for the reader, while at the same time one is conscious that it's not 'really' so.

*

The short story 'Little Tembi' – about a black boy who's first petted, then rejected, and consequently takes to stealing before being delivered to the police – is a slighter variation on the same theme. There, maternal Jane, who once wanted babies so much she could see beyond colour, and for whom Tembi becomes merely a native as he grows up and she has children of her own, is left saying 'restlessly': 'There's something horrible about it all. . . . What is it he was *wanting*, all this time?' (*CAS* 1, p. 123). We are meant to hold Jane responsible: Tembi wants the love and attention she taught him to look for. But he also wants (everyone does) the world, and as a native in this society he is confined to a very small part of it (literally, a prison cell). Jane can't answer her question without undermining her own white identity, so that the issue of responsibility is not just a 'maternal' matter – nor, to put it more politically, a paternalist one. Lessing's self-questioning about the writer's responsibility seems to have been just as uneasy. Her whole treatment of settler society is precisely devoted to doing what her character Jane won't do – un-settling it; but her attempts to represent Africans directly are haunted by the sense that she is behaving, if only metaphorically, like a colonizer, inhabiting their space, claiming to speak for them (the pun implicit in 'represent' is very much to the point here).

In the short story 'The Pig', where the African Jonas uses the gun he has been given for guarding the crops to shoot his young wife's lover, Jonas is made to think with his muscles and in pictures, because Lessing has no words to give him, except for the lie he will tell: that he shot at a pig. The Lessing critic Michael Thorpe suggests that the story 'has a universally intelligible motive' (i.e. jealousy),[11] but Lessing, who is a better cultural historian than that, hints that it is the farmer who – in appointing Jonas as watchman against his own people, in defence of property – has provided the clue for 'jealous' violence. In so far as Africans are accessible to Europeans, they too are often displaced persons. Their heroism or villainy or 'individuality' may be perverse constructs, part projection, part a result of the break-up of tribal life. The novella 'Hunger' suggests as much: that the criminal underworld its hero Jabavu enters in the city, with its violent mutual hatreds, self-hatred and egotism, is a nightmare interval between the collective life of the kraal and the political struggle he will later join. Lessing refers its writing back to a debate during a writers' conference in Moscow in 1952:

> the British . . . agreed . . . that writing had to be a product of the individual conscience or soul. Whereas the Russians did not agree at all. . . . But after all, there was Dickens . . . and his characters were all good or bad – unbelievably Good, monstrously Bad. . . . there I was, with my years in Southern Africa behind me, a society as startlingly unjust as Dickens's England. Why, then, could I not write a story of simple good and bad, with clear-cut choices, set in Africa? (*CAS 2*, 1972 Preface)

The result is a version of urban pastoral, tinged with a dubious nostalgia for the collective conscience (Africans have a clear political destiny). 'The Anthill', another novella, brings some of the ironies into the open. There, a white boy surreptitiously passes on his education to a coloured companion, and they exchange roles, with the European becoming a 'modern' primitive sculptor, and the coloured boy studying law and government, in training for the battle for power.

*

Lessing mapped out the limits of her territory as an 'African' writer with these fables about collective, representative destinies. Marxist thinking about literature during the 1940s had taken as its inspiration the great European novelists who 'were to the bottom of their souls bound up with the movements for the liberation of the people'.[12] But these brave formulas for 'national rebirth' must have acquired an alien colouring in a colonial society, where the communist group was, for most of its members, a fact or a foretaste of exile. Lessing was a transient in Africa. Her heritage was the restlessness that had set her parents' generation on the move: apart from *The Grass is Singing*, almost all of her African writing was done after she arrived in London, a 'reverse immigrant'. The major project by which she planned to write herself out of an African past and into an English present was, of course, the five-novel sequence *Children of Violence* (1952–69), which consisted of *Martha Quest*, *A Proper Marriage*, *A Ripple from the Storm*, *Landlocked* and *The Four-Gated City*. Here she offers a very different kind of 'representative' experience: a study in social, sexual and cultural vagrancy forged out of her own life-history.

The sequence or series format allows for a good deal of wandering, while still holding out the prospect of arrival; it makes space too for the kinds of psycho-historical and social analyses that are crammed into *The Grass is Singing*. It is equally obvious from the beginning of the first of the sequence, *Martha Quest* (1952), however, that there is not as much room for manœuvre as there might seem. Before we have even met Martha, poised at 15 on the threshold of life, we're faced with a daunting epigraph from Olive Schreiner – 'I am so tired of it, and also tired of the future before it comes.' It's a meanly ironic comment on the fossilization of colonial life, so little changed since Schreiner's youth in the last century; and the portrayal of Mr and Mrs Quest bears it out. Their Englishness, his obsession with the Great War ('the Great Unmentionable'), and her nervous, vindictive propriety and ambition, are another variation on the colonial family scenario; so is their vague, genteel rootlessness, their being always about to get off the farm. The quotation from Schreiner anticipates, too, Martha's own bouts of psychic lassitude. In her precocious and rebellious intellectual life she is a sceptical creature of the 1930s who knows about feminism, socialism, internationalism, integration – even adolescence. But this seems to make it harder to take on the future: 'If we *know* it, why do we have to go through the painful business of living it?' (*MQ*, p. 15). She can, though, build a daydream:

> She looked away over the ploughed land, across the veld to the Dumfries Hills, and refashioned that unused country to the scale of her imagination. There arose, glimmering whitely over the harsh scrub and the stunted trees a noble city, set foursquare and colonnaded along its falling flower-bordered terraces. . . . its citizens moved, grave and beautiful, black and white and brown together; and these groups of elders paused, and smiled with pleasure at the sight of the children – the blue-eyed, fair-skinned children of the North playing hand in hand with the bronze-skinned, dark-eyed children of the South . . . (*MQ*, p. 17)

This utopia is an abiding image throughout the *Children of Violence* novels; here it is equally significant that Lessing sardonically 'cuts' straight to 'It was about a year later. Martha was seated beneath the same tree', dreaming the same dream. The druglike sense of sameness traps her on the farm. When she strategically falls ill and refuses more school, it is as much her repeated fantasy of a spacious, unanalysable future as a distaste for her mother's vicarious ambition that explains her inertia.

'Development', then, is a problematic notion, applied to Martha. She does, though, live *serially* – different aspects of her unformed (but already divided) personality take charge at different times. Perhaps the most striking instance of this, apart from the vision of the city, is her experience (one, we're told, she's had before) of an obscure and painful 'ecstasy':

31

There was a slow integration, during which she, and the little animals, and the moving grasses, and the sun-warmed trees, and the slopes of shivering silvery mealies, and the great dome of blue light overhead, and the stones of earth under her feet, became one, shuddering together in a dissolution of dancing atoms. . . . during that space of time (which was timeless) she understood quite finally her smallness, the unimportance of humanity. In her ears was an inchoate grinding, the great wheels of movement . . . and no part of that sound was Martha's voice. Yet she was part of it, reluctantly allowed to participate, though on terms – but what terms? For that moment. . . . she knew futility; that is, what was futile was her own idea of herself and her place in the chaos of matter. What was demanded of her was that she should accept something quite different . . . (*MQ*, p. 62)

'But it did not last.' It is a moment that lies in the narrative like a time bomb, referred to only once again in this novel, to explain what Martha looks for in the books she devours (*MQ*, p. 220; reading too is intense, and intermittent). The suggestion of radical and as yet unimaginable change is left in abeyance, while Martha 'acts' in quite other ways – goes to town, takes a secretarial job, plunges into the life of 'her' generation, centred on the sports club.

The club gets a whole chapter to itself (Part 3, chapter 1) because it represents a collective attempt to evade the past and the unsavoury repressions of the 'British' generation – 'a protest against everything Europe stood for. There were no divisions here, no barriers, or at least none that could be put into words' (*MQ*, p. 154). Sex, drink, clubbable vandalism . . . the suntanned, slangy youth seem to live, in their own way, out of time; even to become in some sort 'African', as they dance themselves into frenzy: 'Perry, apparently, was in a trance of violence. He was letting his shoulders rise and fall convulsively; his eyes rolled to the ceiling, darted sideways with a flash of white eyeball' (*MQ*, p. 176). 'Apparently' is strategically placed: as Martha realizes, the trance is unreal; underneath, the eyes are 'cool and observant' – ' "Look how madly we are behaving," that deep gleam seemed to say.' The club is life suspended. Sexual freedom amounts to mutual masturbation (Martha can lose her virginity only with the pariah Adolf), and when, towards the end of 1938, war in Europe looms, the collective ethos of independence simply evaporates. Marriage spreads like an infection, and glory calls: 'They were saying, devoutly, that things looked like trouble; they did not define this, for it meant what it would have meant to Mr Quest – they would shortly be called on to defend the honour of Britain' (*MQ*, p. 223). Most grotesquely, the always unspoken condition of the club's existence – the act of violence on which the colony is founded – comes to the surface. Perry (in this, the symbol of the gilded youth), after leading a 'native' wardance ('Hold him *down*, the Zulu warrior'), turns to a black waiter and demands that he perform. The scene that follows, where Perry encouragingly demonstrates the dance to the reluctant and gradually terrified waiter, and explodes in martyred fury ('You damned black') as the man escapes, precisely unfolds the conspiracy in which they all live.

Martha lives in it too. Like Lessing's other semi-autobiographical heroines, she is privileged to share in her author's intelligence, energy and ambition, and so privileged to betray herself more absurdly and painfully than her contemporaries. Her 'whirlwind romance' with civil servant Douglas Knowell, a founder member of the club, is banal and self-deceived: she makes him over into a soul-mate in order to marry, like everyone else. Since he reads the *New Statesman*, he must share all her beliefs; with him 'she could be natural'. She was herself – or, rather, 'Herself' as Lessing puts it wryly in the next sentence (*MQ*, p. 239). Even in the breathless interval before their marriage, Martha knows she's wrong. A glimpse of an outdoor socialist meeting, for instance, acts (in a minor way) as another narrative time bomb: for her it is 'rather beautiful'; for the cautious, conformist Douglas, it is an irritation and an anomaly. But their marriage takes place, as if by magic it can dispel all doubt, so that the end of *Martha Quest*,

with the old-fashioned liberal magistrate Mr Maynard left
deploring the irresponsibility of youth, reads like a parody – as
it's meant to – of a nineteenth-century ending. Martha has
hardly begun. What would once have seemed a definitive
choice now is not. Choice itself, for her, has become suspect,
unreal – at least in so far as it is supposed to imply a whole
individual action that proceeds from a whole personality. Like
her contemporaries (like her parents?), she is meshed in contra-
diction.

As she saw before the era of the club, in the colony 'each
group, community, clan, colour, strove and fought away from
each other, in a sickness of dissolution . . . as if the principle of
separateness was bred from the very soil' (MQ, p. 56). Men's
eyes tell the tale: 'There is a pale and fretful look; the soft and
luminous darkness that should lie behind the iris is simply not
there. Something is missing' (MQ, p. 58). At the club, too, she
becomes 'obsessed with the need to look at the eyes of these
people. . . . It was as if their surface, their limbs, their voices
were possessed' (MQ, p. 172). But it's not just a matter of eyes:
there has all along been a pervasive shiftiness in people's
behaviour that deflects one's attention from what they mean,
or think they mean, to a different, buried message. Mrs Quest's
resigned sigh, for instance:

> The sigh, it appeared, had the power to reach where her
> words could not. Both Martha and Mr Quest glanced up,
> guiltily. Mrs Quest had forgotten them . . . was twiddling a
> lock of that limp grey hair round and round one finger – a
> mannerism which always stung Mr Quest – while with the
> other hand she stroked her skirt, in a tired, hard, nervous
> movement which affected Martha like a direct criticism of
> ingratitude. (MQ, p. 70)

This is, as it were, the atmosphere in which words and events
exist in the *Children of Violence* sequence, and it thickens in
each novel, so that *A Proper Marriage* (1954) seems to begin
with an atavistic mime – the men spoiling for war, the women
drifting resentfully into pregnancy. But the body language and

34

the eye language are more complex than that. Precisely because they betray unease, they are also a means of controlling and directing it. Thus it is established at a smart party, through eye contact and silence, that 'kaffirs' and 'niggers' are now – given the state of emergency – to be upgraded to 'natives'. Martha, prompted by Mr Maynard, begins to cultivate an 'enjoyable cynicism' ('the more things change, the more they remain the same'; *PM*, p. 67) which turns to nightmare when she suspects she is pregnant, and sees herself passing on her mother's self-deception and bitterness: 'This . . . the nightmare of a class and generation: repetition. . . . a series of doomed individuals, carrying their doom *inside* them' (*PM*, p. 109). On the local narrative scale, bad faith seems unavoidable. Lessing the narrator reinforces Mr Maynard's tone: 'Someone has remarked that there is no such thing as a hypocrite. In order to believe that, one must have reached the age to understand how persistently one has not been a hypocrite oneself' (*PM*, p. 97). Or again, 'There is no such thing as a female hypocrite' (*PM*, p. 199).

This is the nearest way to make sense of Martha's contradictions (and not only hers); but it's not the only one. Accompanying it is another, larger-scale narrative that sets off the explosive trail laid in the first novel. The moment during Martha's pregnancy when she wallows naked in a rainstorm in a pothole in the veld comes from this other story; and so does her long-postponed love-affair with radicalism. It is the clash between her two stories – growth versus repetition – that provokes her moment of choice:

> Suddenly . . . that feeling of staleness came over her, a sort of derisive boredom. . . . the enemy which made any kind of enthusiasm or idealism ridiculous.
>
> The life she was living seemed dignified and attractive. But no sooner had she come to this conclusion than disgust rose against it; and she thought with tender longing of these new possibilities. . . . Yet almost at once . . . derision arose, that stale disgust. (*PM*, pp. 307–8)

It is less a choice than an exorcism. 'With one sudden move-ment of her whole being' (again, a move that belongs to the 'explosive' narrative) she commits herself: 'it was like a re-birth' (*PM*, p. 315). Her marriage breaks up amid false drama and play-acting, the perfection of bad faith.

Mr Maynard admits defeat ('I suppose with the French Revolution for a father and the Russian Revolution for a mother, you can very well dispense with a family'; *PM*, p. 380), and the idiom of growth is in control. And yet, already, even before the end, we're aware that the communist group is as socially and sexually complicated as the maze from which she has extricated herself; and that Martha is again deceiving herself when she claims she's not leaving Douglas for anyone: 'she saw Anton Hesse in her mind's eye and brought out aggressively, "I'm going to live differently" ' (*PM*, p. 353). Thus, it is hardly a surprise that the opening pages of the third novel in the sequence, *A Ripple from the Storm* (1958), discover Martha reflecting: 'The shortest acquaintance with politics should be enough to teach anyone that listening to the words people use is the longest way around to an understanding of what is going on' (*RS*, p. 13). The whole business of reading people's dividedness and dis-ease (it amounts to that) has begun again. The glimmering utopian city has in a sense drawn nearer: watching a ragged black boy in the street, Martha and Jasmine, united by the group, can share a vision: 'Each saw an ideal town, clean, noble, and beautiful, soaring up over the actual town. . . . The ragged child was already a citizen . . . co-citizen with themselves' (*RS*, p. 34). Anton Hesse's imper-sonal 'calm voice' piecing together a communist world-picture links Martha 'with those parts of her childhood she still owned . . . the moments of illumination and belief' (*RS*, p. 62). But the narrative, tied here more insistently than in the earlier two novels to local detail, implicitly satirizes both the unity of the group and its claims to vision. The shifting loyalties, the sexual pressures, the uneasy jokes – all conspire to reveal it, with depressing clarity, as a rootless, transient configuration thrown up by the war, and insulated from the black population. In short, it begins in some awful way – though nothing openly prompts the reader to this – to resemble the club. And Martha begins to resemble her earlier self:

> She thought: and it was a moment of illumination, a flash of light: I don't know anything about anything yet. I must try and keep myself free and open, and try to think more, try not to drift into things. (*RS*, p. 186)

Almost immediately she drifts into marriage with Anton (things have speeded up) – ostensibly to save him from internment, actually because it's in the air. Facing her mirror on their wedding morning, she rehearses her story with incredulity:

> She examined the severe young face and thought: If I didn't know myself, what would I think? Well, I certainly wouldn't guess all the things that have happened to *her* in the last year, getting divorced, being a communist, getting married again, all the complications and never sleeping enough. (*RS*, p. 193)

As she did once before, she is marrying a vision of community and wholeness in a man who has already repelled and disappointed her.

*A Ripple from the Storm* takes her back to a beginning – 'The fact is, I'm not a person at all, I'm nothing yet – perhaps I never will be' (*RS*, p. 279) – but narratively it has exhausted the stores of 'illumination' that lent a parodic upbeat to the unhappy ending of *Martha Quest*. The inward disintegration of the group, and the split in the Labour Party over African membership, give Martha's 'nothing yet' a context of general defeat. Perhaps the cruellest gesture, though, is the portrayal of Mrs Van, the powerful and admirable Labour matron who has replaced Mr Maynard as a possible model of how to live with the colony, but who is seen, in all her humanity and competence, as hiding the secret wrong of a 'sensible' marriage: 'She talked on in a harsh wondering voice. Her small blue eyes moved from one article of furniture to another and her hands plucked at her dress until at last the servant came in' (*RS*, p. 245). This reminder of Mrs Quest is, and is intended to be, deeply depressing. The way to the future is barred by past failures, whose true nature remains stubbornly unresolved. The last section's epigraph from Marx – 'The origin of states gets lost in a myth in which one may believe but one may not discuss' – says the same thing, on a grander level. So, although the world is still all before Martha, the further she goes, it seems, the less she possesses herself, and the more she reflects the disintegration around her. *Children of Violence*, so far, is a reluctantly ironic demonstration that in a culture based on a gigantic cover-up (race, sex) you cannot achieve a 'whole' identity. However, the irony is felt as a defeat, not a solution. As Dagmar Barnouw very rightly says: 'Matty is neither moving toward a choice, a determining decision she will make at one time or the other, nor is the fact that she is incapable of such a choice integrated into the substance and structure of her development.'[13] The visionary illuminations implied some other end, but in *A Ripple from the Storm* the narrative has 'settled' into a weary close-up focus.

It was at this point, poised to follow the process of Martha's exile from the colony, that Lessing turned aside from *Children of Violence*. Exile had to mean more than it seemed likely to in this dry idiom. Martha is accused by her creator (and herself) of drifting, lying, playing parts. But perhaps this is as much a product of the point of view from which she's seen, as of her 'character' – which is still, Lessing wants to insist, an open question. So she turned around to explore her own relation as writer to the materials of her writing. *The Golden Notebook* (1962), set in London in 1957, took the narrative process apart and laid it out, to find a new beginning. And this, really, was the point at which her own exile from Africa *as a writer* occurred. When she returned to *Children of Violence* with *Landlocked* (1965), it was the pull of the future rather than the impetus of the past that was structuring Martha's destiny. *The Golden Notebook* forced a crisis – a new displacement, displacement squared.

38

# 2

## ENGLAND

Doris Lessing had arrived in London 'in 1949, when England was at its dingiest, my personal fortunes at their lowest, and my morale at zero. I also had a small child' (*IPE*, p. 14). However, *The Grass is Singing* quickly found a publisher. She had become a writer, and, for almost ten years, she wrote herself out of Africa, while gradually and rather reluctantly acclimatizing herself in England. It was – she told C. J. Driver[14] – her family's doubtful Englishness rather than any international communist contacts that enabled her to adapt; she did not join the British Communist Party until 1952, and left it in 1956. The change in material circumstance and culture was troubled, and a general air of dubiety and unease hangs over the English writings from these years. Nearly all are uncharacteristically glum and hesitant: the novella 'The Other Woman', collected in 1953 with four African novellas to make *Five*; the unsuccessful 'exile' romance *Retreat to Innocence* (1956); the stories collected in *The Habit of Loving* in 1957, the year also of her essay on the state of the novel, 'The Small Personal Voice', which is rather more deliberately hopeful and international in tone; a play and some poems; and, effectively summing up this whole period, her documentary book *In Pursuit of the English* (1960).

This last work typifies the whole experience, with its wry confession that the English have been hard to find: 'like Bushmen in the Kalahari, that doomed race, they vanish into camouflage at the first sign of a stranger' (*IPE*, p. 7). And, though her 'mentors' had claimed 'that not one truthful word could ever be written unless it was first baptized, so to speak, by the working class' (*IPE*, p. 10), the working class have proved even more elusive. Political judgements would not settle easily, and London at first was a grey mirage of destruction and decay in this post-war time, which took on life only when she managed to glimpse Africa beyond it:

> Sometimes it was as if the walls dissolved, and I was left sitting under a tree, listening to birds talking from branch to branch until the last fat drops of a shower spattered on the leaves. . . . Sometimes I put my ear to the wall and heard how, as the trains went past and the buses rocked their weight along the street, shock after shock came up through brick and plaster, so that the solid walls had the fluidity of dancing atoms, and I felt the house, the street, the pavement, and all the miles and miles of houses and streets as a pattern of magical balances, a weightless structure, as if this city hung on water or on sound. (*IPE*, pp. 79–80)

Later she was to recognize, in the working men patching up the war damage and papering over the cracks, the same passive resistance to their lot – the same 'accomplished idling' (*IPE*, p. 206) – as she'd seen in Africans. Here, though, much more depressingly, resistance signified that the 'new' Labour bureaucracy had really changed nothing. People seemed passive, privatized, defeated – most particularly her friend Rose, who had become for Lessing almost the embodiment of disaffection. Rose shared with London's cynical rebuilders a dull anger against all political abstractions and do-gooding 'nosey parkers', but took a bitter pride in hard work. Rose contrived and saved; her anxiety for security was slowly killing her sexuality; and – final irony – she'd come to look back on the war as the only time when things did change, when 'people liked each other' (*IPE*, p. 114). Another Rose in 'The Other Woman' was given many of the documentary Rose's idioms – 'Don't make me laugh', 'They make me sick', and the polite 'Yes?', 'sceptical and dismissing', that acts as 'a statement of rock-bottom disbelief' (*CS* 1, pp. 99, 129). This fictional Rose, stunned into defensive dread by her parents' deaths (a street accident, the blitz), gives up on love to lodge with her lover's ex-wife, and to adopt an old boyfriend's orphaned child, desperately piecing together a future. They are to live in a basement – a version of the buried, 'bomb-proof' existence to which Lessing felt the English were retreating.

For the most part, her 1950s English fiction reflected her own uprooted state – *Retreat to Innocence* in particular, which she herself has acknowledged is a failure, and encouraged (apart from one paperback reprinting) to drift into oblivion. Not, one suspects, out of purely writerly pride (since she is usually, as in the prefaces to the collected stories, indulgent towards failures in that direction, like 'Hunger') but because it represents a rare loss of conviction on her part: an attempt at a self-contained, neat, impersonal novel. An English novel, in short – but one conceived by a writer who regarded such a project with a kind of despairing contempt. Thus, English novels mainly being middle class, she invents a heroine, Julia Barr, whose father is a dimly conceived Norfolk baronet of liberal persuasions; England being frigidly conventional, Julia is given a boyfriend who is a prig working for the Home Office, and whom Lessing hardly has the patience to characterize further. Julia herself fares little better, though the narrative is filtered through her self-regarding, spoilt-girl's consciousness.

The plot brings this conventional heroine up against a middle-aged Czech refugee writer, Jan Brod, who represents – in his peasant Jewishness and his ambivalent love-affair with the communist cause – all the mess of history on which her 1950s generation had turned its back ('I loathe politics. I hate them. All my generation do. All that filth and dirt and heroics'; *RI*, p. 38). Jan is spectacularly un-English, indecorous, vagrant, ironic, and regularly rejected in his applications for British citizenship by the Home Office. Their affair thus dramatizes a small breach in English 'innocence' (in the form of Julia's virginity, political and otherwise) before the plot sends them off in their separate directions – he to return 'home' in the spirit of sceptical resignation, she to marry her civil servant. And this is the other implication of the novel's title: that the mid-1950s are years of moral exhaustion, when people opt for compromise, simplification, degrees of unfreedom.

Lessing was clearly tired too. Perhaps the novel's most telling motif is Jan Brod's own long-laboured novel, which he dismisses as a failure, and which sounds very like an apologia for Stalin:

> 'Imagine – he lay there, and looked at them, and he thought: Because of me, your hands are clean. My hands are red, but it's on your account. . . . There can have been no man in the whole history of the world as lonely as that man when he died.' (*RI*, p. 274)

This, one imagines, was the communist epic that Lessing, by 1955, had come to regard with a mixture of nostalgia, dread and deep embarrassment. Certainly it much resembles the Communist Party fantasies she later anatomizes so mercilessly in the 'Red' sections of *The Golden Notebook*.

On the other hand, she could not, any more than her character Jan Brod, make herself at home with the tone of British culture in the 1950s. Like *Retreat to Innocence*, many of the stories deal with 'exiled' characters – often the British abroad, ominously reaffirming their insularity. The most ambitious of these, 'The Habit of Loving', sketches a whole decade in the life of George Talbot, an ageing man of the theatre, whose attempt to recapture his cosmopolitan assurance after the war, and after a broken love-affair, introduces him to a new brand of role-playing, suited to the contemporary climate of scepticism. Bobby, the 35-year-old 'boyish' cabaret artist he marries, is far more *déclassé* and versatile than the Roses (Bobby is camp Cockney), but like them she has a 'rock-bottom disbelief' which foils George's efforts at romantic seduction (the honeymoon in France, the practised love-making). When she goes back to work, he begins to see why. Her act – shared with a male 'double' – is part of a fashionable revue that travesties historical heroics and romantic emotionalism:

George felt all his responses blocked, first because he could not allow himself to feel any emotion from that time at all – it was too painful; and then because of the five-finger-exercise style, which contradicted everything, all pain or protest, leaving nothing. . . . that insane nihilistic music demanded some opposition, some statement of affirmation, but the two urchins, half-boy, half-girl, as alike as twins . . . were not even trying to resist. . . . the limp sadness of the turn was unbearable . . . (*CS* 1, pp. 25–7)

Bobby's self-punishing love is reserved for the youthful other half of her act ('He does not love me. . . . I could 'ave bin 'is muvver, see?'; *CS* 1, p. 31). She celebrates her fortieth birthday by presenting herself to George as a carbon copy of her older sister Rosa, 'a commonplace, middle-aged female from some suburb' (*CS* 1, p. 21), thus neatly revealing the kinship in Lessing's imagination between the sterility of smart parody and that of dull disaffection. *In Pursuit of the English*, too, ends with a specimen of 'new' 1950s parodic humour, in Rose's vaguely criminal younger brother, with his zany, oblivious backchat.

\*

In these years, then, Lessing found herself confronting both the ironic impasse she had reached in *Children of Violence* (Martha back to square one, 'nothing yet') and this – to her – dismayingly blocked, passive British post-war culture. Her plea for 'realism' and 'humanism' in 'The Small Personal Voice' recovers its defiant tone in this context (one should remember too that she'd left the Communist Party shortly before):

I believe that the pleasurable luxury of despair, the acceptance of disgust, is as much a betrayal of what a writer should be as the acceptance of the simple economic view of man. . . . They are opposite sides of the same coin. One sees man as the isolated individual unable to communicate, helpless and solitary; the other as collective man with a collective conscience. Somewhere between these two, I believe, is a resting point, a place of decision, hard to reach and precariously balanced.[15]

By 'despair', though, she meant Camus, Sartre, Genet, Beckett; in Britain writers cultivated a more provincial, 'derisive' style of disillusion. The 'Angry Young Men' (she was writing for an anthology that included John Osborne, Colin Wilson and John Wain) were neither rebels nor outsiders from her point of view, but in the most depressing sense *insiders* – 'their horizons are bounded by their immediate experience of British life and standards'. The cold war has made the communist third of the world unimaginable; the nightmare threat of nuclear war has made a paralysing gap between the private and the public conscience: 'Thinking internationally means choosing a particular shade of half-envious, half-patronizing emotion to feel about the United States; or collecting money for Hungary, or taking little holidays in Europe, or liking French or Italian films.' Her scorn is fuelled by an impatient yearning (compare her creature Martha's 'moments of illumination and belief') for membership of the wider, changeful world. The climactic restatement of her credo gathers its force from the old vision of the writer as truly 'representative':

> we are all of us, directly or indirectly, caught up in a great whirlwind of change; and I believe that if an artist has once felt this, in himself . . . it is an end of despair, and the aridity of self-pity. It is the beginning of something else which I think is the minimum act of humility for a writer: to know that one is a writer at all because one represents, makes articulate, is continuously and invisibly fed by, numbers of people who are inarticulate, to whom one belongs, to whom one is responsible.

The 'great whirlwind of change' here recalls 'the great wheels of movement' on which Martha eavesdropped, the experience she used as her 'tuning fork or guide' in her reading:

> that knowledge of something painful and ecstatic, some-

44

thing central and fixed, but flowing. It was a sense of movement, of separate things interacting and finally becoming one, but greater – it was this which was her lodestone, even her conscience . . . (*MQ*, p. 220)

However, this vivid sense of the writer's relation to the collective life, which pre-dated and (this is one of the essay's main points) outlived Lessing's communism, was also deeply problematic. It had become a buried theme in her fiction, overlaid with the small change of change, as it were – manners and mores.

In some ways, too, the essay is misleading. The 'realism' Lessing was talking about had always implied for her a set of values, an ideology. She was appealing, certainly, to a tradition and a cluster of stylistic strategies inherited from the nineteenth century, but she read that tradition in the way it had long been read in Marxist circles – as a radical and in some sort revolutionary one. Rather, for instance, as a critic like Raymond Williams did in *The Long Revolution* in 1961. His carefully moderate account there of the history of the novel attempts, like 'The Small Personal Voice', to trace a structural connection between a holistic 'realism' and a revolutionary history:

> a particular apprehension of a relation between individuals and society. . . . this viewpoint was itself the product of maturity; the history of the novel from the eighteenth century is essentially an exploration towards this position. . . . Reality is continually established, by common effort, and art is one of the highest forms of this process. Yet the tension can be great . . . and many kinds of failure and breakdown are possible. It seems to me that in a period of exceptional growth, as ours has been and will continue to be, the tension will be exceptionally high, and certain kinds of failure and breakdown may become characteristic.[16]

Williams here might almost have been outlining a synopsis for *The Golden Notebook*. He and Lessing overlap so closely, not by virtue of any particular influence one way or another, but because they share the assumptions of the Marxist Left. However, in one all-important direction, Lessing was to part company with Williams, and with her own credo in 'The Small Personal Voice'. 'Breakdown' became a positive value in her writing, an authentic response to what Williams tactfully calls 'a period of exceptional growth' – the period when, for her as for many who left the Communist Party, history was suddenly structureless.

The problem begins to unfold itself if one looks again at her gloss on the word 'represents': 'makes articulate, is continuously and invisibly fed by'. It was this conviction that the realist writer is not a representational artist but a *representative* that was to take her, in *The Golden Notebook* (1962), into the heart of the most complex post-war debates on the novel, in the novel. The French *nouveau roman* and novels about novels were remote from her sympathies. None the less – and despite her contempt for 'isms' – she too stepped through the looking-glass to question the conventions she'd been working with. She had long been hypersensitive – thanks to the colony – to the way cultures establish what is and is not 'real'. She had, though, seen art, and the novel in particular, as on the side of light in this matter; whereas now she questioned whether the density and specificity of 'character' and 'plot', and the pictorial assumptions that adhered to conventional realism, were not themselves dangerously inert. And this takes her into the territory of Nathalie Sarraute, or Phillippe Sollers:

> Our identity depends on the novel, what others think of us, what we think of ourselves, the way in which our life is imperceptibly moulded into a whole. How do others see us if not as a character from a novel?[17]

Sollers's tone (he takes our living in fictions very coolly) is a world away from Lessing's, but his question is very much to the point. In *Children of Violence* she had been on the brink of metafiction: Martha, for instance, is not only a character in a novel; she *acts like* a character in a novel, at the expense of her freedom. The body language and eye language that contradict other characters' presentations of themselves, too, hint at a fluidity underlying their 'personalities'. Conventionally, one would take this as a sign of the psychological damage caused by their society; however, it also questions the narrative's own production of personality. The habitual repressions of the colony and 'realist' habits of representation may have something nastily in common. It is often remarked that the novel is middle class; it could as well be said that it is a colonizing genre (think of *Robinson Crusoe*) that crowds out other possible world-pictures.

Lessing would not put it this way. But her practice suggests, again and again, that she had arrived at what Sarraute called 'the age of suspicion'. Consider this portrait of Mr Maynard:

> The man was tall, rather heavy; the grey flannel which encased him was like a firm outer skin to his assurance. His large elderly face had the authority of a commanding nose, jowled cheeks, strong hazel eyes deep under thick black brows. It was that English face which, with various small deviations, has been looking down so long from the walls and countless picture galleries of country houses. Handsome it was, but more – every feature, every curve, had an impressive finality, an absolute rightness, as if the atoms which composed it had never a moment's hesitation in falling where they did. (*PM*, p. 10)

This is the set-piece *as* set-piece: Mr Maynard's 'finality' includes a recognition that description of this traditional kind tends towards producing not persons but personages, authority figures who imply wholeness and order as an ideal. Sarraute's *Martereau* (1953) takes such a figure (he's even felt to be peculiarly English) and shows how, just by existing, he acts as a picturesque protector against a threatening swarm of subjective uncertainties. Hélène Cixous's savage theoretical attack on character extends the argument:

> In this system, the 'character' represents a set of externals. . . . the guarantor of the transmission of sense and of

47

the 'true', at once *porte-parole*, emissary, and idol, indubitably human, at least partially universalizable, and homogeneous.

> The ideology underlying this fetishization of 'character' is that of an 'I' who is a *whole* subject . . . conscious, knowable.[18]

It is Mr Maynard, of course, who tries to make Martha share in his ironic certainty that 'the more things change, the more they remain the same'.

To be 'representative', though, was not necessarily to be representational. Lessing came back to this, and to the problem she'd faced but not solved in *The Grass is Singing* at the beginning of her writing career. Representing Moses had never been a question of writing *about* him (see pp. 26–8) but of speaking for him in some way that wouldn't write/white him out. Martha Quest's illumination is again to the point: 'no part of that sound was Martha's voice. Yet she was part of it, reluctantly allowed to participate. . . . what was futile was her own idea of herself and her place in the chaos of matter' (*MQ*, p. 62). Somewhere in the uncharacterizable regions of the psyche lies a kind of answer – but not, as in *The Grass is Singing*, one that can be articulated in a conventional narrative. Mary Turner's dissolution must first become her author's; she must ask herself (in Hélène Cixous's words): 'Who am I when I am you, you, or him, and pretty far away from myself?'[19] And so, like so many of her post-war (but not, usually, British) contemporaries, Lessing moved to deconstruct the narrator and the narrative process. She would have said 'to analyse', in something like the psychoanalytic sense, since the realist *project* remained as imperative as ever. And for this reason it is perhaps better to describe what she's doing in *The Golden Notebook* as a new stage in 'un-settlement' or 'decolonization'. This formulation at least reminds one how thoroughly the novel as a form is, for her, an aspect of the making of a wider history; and how problematic her Englishness had turned out to be.

\*

The structure of *The Golden Notebook* – the containing, conventional novel 'Free Women', intercut with the four 'notebooks' that explore the underlying chaos of relations between sexual and political experience and creativity – is elaborately and deliberately orchestrated. More so, in fact, than anything Lessing had done since her first novel. This time, however, the planning is reflexive: blocked feeling has become writer's block; the breakdown is the artist's; and the repressions and gaps belong not only to an alien culture but to the storytelling process. The new heroine, Anna Wulf, shares some of Martha's experience (she lived in Rhodesia during the war, and was part of a communist group), but she has no past to speak of. Instead she is caught in a hall of mirrors: the African experience she made over into a bestseller called *Frontiers of War* (now anatomized in the Black Notebook); her painful withdrawal from the communist 'myth' (the Red Notebook); abortive storytelling, projected on to a fictional 'Ella', also a blocked novelist (the Yellow Notebook); and a diary of sorts, a private extension of her psychoanalysis with the jokily named Mrs Marks (the Blue Notebook). Anna has divided herself up this way, we're told, in order to register her chaos, and stave it off. On the surface, her story is that of 'Free Women', a wry tale that keeps her in middle-distance focus, as much involved in others' lives as in her own. It is a version of the 'resting point' between the individual and the collective Lessing had talked about in 'The Small Personal Voice', but in the context of the notebooks it is clearly about exhaustion. Most readers probably begin by accepting it as realistic. And in a sense it is.

The tone is reluctantly ironic: Anna and her friend Molly are women escaped from marriage, bringing up children alone, but hardly 'free' from men (their friendship consists partly of supporting each other in the face of repeated disappointments); when they meet after a year, Anna finds herself inwardly rebelling, foreseeing a spinsterly anecdotage for the two of them:

if I'm not careful, Molly and I will descend into a kind of twin old-maidhood, where we sit around saying to each other, Do you remember how that man, what-was-his-name said that insensitive thing, it must have been in 1947 . . . (*GN*, p. 53)

It has come to seem to her that, while their shared tone does indeed enable them to carry on, that is precisely what is wrong with it. But this dangerous perception can only express itself, in 'Free Women', as the kind of dis-ease that had taken over in *Children of Violence* – Molly's hands unconsciously twisting and pleading, Anna blackmailed back into the 'safe tone' ('Yes, it's all very odd . . . well, I must be rushing home'; *GN*, p. 59). The shareable language shuts out the possibility of breakdown, of radical discontinuity. And, as we come to realize, this is partly why Anna can't write any longer, because fiction too seems to involve a lying, self-preserving collusion. Her note-books (private anti-writing) try to unravel the comforting ironies.

In the Black Notebook she convicts herself of having mere-triciously written up Africa in '*Frontiers of War*'. It's not just that the novel – a 'colour bar' romance about a British airman and an African girl – rearranged events picturesquely (though we're told it did: actually what she remembers is at once more banal and more tangled) but that it was tainted unawares with what she now recognizes as a kind of nihilism, bred out of the war, and out of the impossibility of really imagining change in the colony. A comforting nihilism, though, not unrelated to her tone with Molly:

> I hate that tone, and yet we all lived inside it for months and years. . . . It was self-punishing, a locking of feeling, an inability or a refusal to fit conflicting things together to make a whole; so that one can live inside it, no matter how terrible. The refusal means one can neither change nor destroy . . . (*GN*, p. 72)

To underline the point, this first chunk of the Black Notebook – a vividly 'realist' rendering of the sexual and social dynamics of the communist group, and of the horrible ineptitude of their ventures across the colour bar – is dismissed as 'nostalgic', lying. The reasons for this deception are complicated, as the impatient, ambiguous syntax of the quotation above implies: the 'it' ('one can live inside it') ought, in a world of continuities, to refer to 'a whole', but here turns out to mean the rejected 'tone'. It's by refusing 'to fit conflicting things together' that you make yourself a refuge to 'live inside'. But surely (Anna begins to realize) you do this because, if you do fit things together, the 'whole' they make is chaos? The notebooks stop halfway, but, as they add up, that is their message. The Red Notebook shows the Communist Party in the same hard focus, buoyed up in its statutory Stalinism by self-censorship and jokes. And again she's brought back to the brink of meaninglessness:

> somewhere at the back of my mind when I joined the Party was a need for wholeness, for an end to the split, divided, unsatisfactory way we all live. Yet joining the Party intensified the split – not the business of belonging to an organization whose every tenet, on paper, anyway, contradicts the ideas of the society we live in; but something much deeper than that. (GN, p. 162)

Her sense of what 'wholeness' might consist in is undergoing a traumatic revision. Or, to put it another way, she's cracking up.

The most damaging and demoralizing split is the sexual one, worked out by Anna in the fiction-within-a-fiction of Ella and Paul in the Yellow Notebook. By making Ella at once a writer, and the surrogate for her sexual self (Paul mirrors Anna's lover Michael, whom we hear little about in 'Free Women'), the Yellow Notebook brings chaos very close to home. Paul, for Ella, has been a 'real man'; her own sensations prove it: 'the orgasm that is created by the man's need for a woman, and his confidence in that need. . . . The vaginal orgasm is a dissolving in a vague, dark generalized sensation like being swirled in a warm whirlpool' (GN, pp. 212–13). But these very sensations are called into question when the focus of their love-making shifts from what she 'insisted on calling "a real orgasm"' to the

51

clitoral orgasm. As he tries to tell her, there is 'no physical basis' for her blissful loss of self; and, as she comes to see, there's no psychological basis for her insistence that he is a 'real man' either. Paul is a conglomeration of bitterly inconsistent persons, as is Ella, and he resents her when she tries to put him together. When he leaves her, refuses finally to be 'real', she plummets into self-doubt and self-consciousness: '*What Ella lost during those five years was the power to create through naivety*' (*GN*, p. 209). Paul's ironic recognition of the shape of things to come ('The real revolution is, women against men' (*GN*, p. 211), though he was wiser than he or Lessing knew, as we shall see) strikes Ella as a betrayal: 'that is why you'll ultimately turn out to be unnecessary – because you haven't got any faith in what you are' (*GN*, p. 211). His 'faith' was supposed to complete her, and his desertion leaves her self-divided. The Blue Notebook, back with Anna, summing up the first sequence, shows her offering her analyst Mrs Marks an allegorical dream of a casket full of fragments:

> Not a whole thing, broken into fragments, but bits and pieces from everywhere, all over the world . . . a lump of red earth . . . from Africa, and then a bit of metal that came off a gun from Indo-China . . . bits of flesh from people killed in the Korean War and a communist party badge off someone who died in a Soviet prison. (*GN*, p. 247)

In the dream these horrors are metamorphosed into 'a small green crocodile with a winking sardonic snout' that cries diamond tears and delights the money-people. We're back, seemingly, to the meretricious, nihilistic tone of which she'd accused herself (and her bestseller) in the Black Notebook.

The second section of 'Free Women' has Anna trying to talk sanity to Molly's sick and hysterical adolescent son Tommy, and failing. He's eavesdropped on her notebooks, and knows she's lying: 'If things are a chaos, then that's what they are' (*GN*, p. 268). Having 'exposed' her (and through her his mother), he attempts suicide. This is the central event of 'Free Women', and, for all its vividness, it is a measure of how far

Anna's wretchedness is displaced to make a public plot about the failure of idealism. In the notebooks nothing so dreadful happens to Tommy (he drifts more or less cynically into the 'New Left'); the disasters happen, implosively, to Anna, as her fear grows and the entries become more and more fragmented. But just as it was the Yellow Notebook that left her most stripped of assurance, it is there too that dividedness takes on a new meaning. Ella wakes out of her old reverie ('A woman's sexuality is . . . contained by a man, if he is a real man'; *GN*, p. 447) to invent a new scenario:

> I've got to accept the patterns of self-knowledge which mean unhappiness or at least a dryness. But I can twist it into victory. A man and a woman – yes. Both at the end of their tether. Both cracking up because of a deliberate attempt to transcend their own limits. And out of the chaos, a new kind of strength. (*GN*, p. 458)

This project seeps, as it were, back into Anna's life. In the Blue Notebook she remembers having said to Mrs Marks that instead of assimilating her experience to the communality of myth (another fake refuge) she should be on the lookout for anomalies:

> if I'd said to you . . . : yesterday I met a man at a party and I recognized in him the wolf, or the knight . . . you'd nod and you'd smile. . . . But if I'd said . . . : *Yes*, there's a hint of something – there's a crack in that man's personality like a gap in a dam, and through that gap the future might pour . . . (*GN*, pp. 463–4)

There's a new-old dream that goes with this: a vicious, grotesque dwarf, double-sexed or sexless, the principle of 'joy in spite', a dream Anna has always had when 'the walls of myself were thin or in danger' (*GN*, pp. 467–8). Half consciously she's invoking the chaos and violence the notebooks have compartmentalized.

Meanwhile 'Free Women' papers over the cracks. Tommy has lost his sight, and his vision of chaos. Lives rearrange themselves in 'odd' patterns: Tommy living with his step-mother; Anna's young daughter, on her own insistence, attending the most conventional of boarding schools; Anna and Molly each isolated in pointless 'freedom'. It is to be the story of an ironic defeat. But underground the notebooks, merging one into another, are – in Ella's phrase – twisting it into victory. The man in her scenario, the hypothetical man at the party, materializes in the American Saul Green, cold war veteran, womanizer, vagrant and, like Anna, on the edge of madness. He suits her now, an unreal, lost man wandering from one persona into another before her eyes, daring her into craziness. And their mutual disintegration – in a savage paradox – puts them suddenly at the centre of their world:

> I was desperately ashamed, being locked in Anna's, an unimportant little animal's terrors. I kept saying to myself: Out there is the world. . . . I fetched the week's newspapers. . . . The feeling of banality, the disgust of banality . . . and then suddenly I moved forward into a new knowledge. . . . There was a kind of shifting of the balances of my brain, of the way I had been thinking, the same kind of realignment as when, a few days before, words like democracy, liberty, freedom, had faded under pressure of a new sort of understanding of the real movement of the world towards dark, hardening power. I *knew* . . . that whatever already is has its logic and its force, that the great armouries of the world have their inner force, and that my terror . . . was part of the force. . . . And I knew that the cruelty and the spite and the I, I, I, I, of Saul and Anna were part of the logic of war . . . (*GN*, pp. 575–6)

Near the beginning of the novel, Anna had confessed to 'torments of dissatisfaction and incompletion because of my inability to enter those ways of life my way of living, education, sex, politics, class bar me from' (*GN*, p. 68). Now those barriers are down, for 'ways of life' have dissolved into a much more primitive and desperate striving. Her Golden Notebook – a fifth one, superseding the others – is no longer hers: 'if there were a tape . . . of the hours and hours of talk in that room . . . it would be a record of a hundred different people living now, in various parts of the world, talking and crying out and question-ing' (*GN*, p. 608). She and Saul, letting their bitterness and incoherence flow over them like tides, have been crucially un-settled, scattered into near-anonymity. As Lessing says in her Preface, the Golden Notebook, with its babble of voices, is 'written by both of them': 'you can no longer distinguish between what is Saul and what is Anna'. When they part, they act out this nearly 'anonymous' creativity by giving each other opening sentences for new novels. Saul's offering (for Anna) is the first sentence of *The Golden Notebook*, the novel that is made whole by the acceptance of disintegration.

This, however, is not the end. The final 'Free Women' section has its Anna (after an encounter with a much less crazy American called Milt) precisely not writing the novel (this novel) but going off (wryly) into marriage guidance and the Labour Party. The author and the persona part company, to remind us that the containing fiction *merely* contains, and that the 'character' Anna is held together by conventional realist glue, as well as stoicism. In effect, Lessing has produced what geometricians would call an impossible object, for the 'inner' space of the notebooks also contains its outer envelope. She has set realist ends (speaking for/to others) against realist means (the conventional narrative of 'Free Women'). Most particu-larly, she has jettisoned the assumption that the individual personality is sacred. These moves bring her long engagement with the realist tradition to crisis point. If there was an 'ex-plosive' subtext in the first three novels of *Children of Violence*, here the bomb has dropped. (Lessing indeed talked a great deal during these years about the slow detonation of the meaning of the atomic bomb in people's minds, and saw it as an ironic proof of the final unity of human destinies.) The amorphous, anonymous voices of 'breakdown' now stand – by a violent paradox – for wholeness.

*The Golden Notebook* was a momentous book – a book *of* its moment, opened up to subconscious and subcultural imperatives which the realist perspective had structured and suppressed. Because Lessing had found a form that so exactly focused her struggles with/against realism, it was a novel that persuaded its readers of the limitations of that shared language more painfully, and even perhaps more intimately, than French new novels, or than anti-realist writing from America. Sarraute and Robbe-Grillet began from the culture of the unreal, the sub-real; Barth and Pynchon were reflexive jokers from the start. But Lessing worked her passage, as it were, and documented the voyage. And the result was that she did what many of her 'experimental' contemporaries claimed, but failed, to do – produced a novel that unravelled itself in its readers' responses in altogether unexpected ways. She had 'represented' them better than she knew.

Women, in particular, appropriated her voice. *The Golden Notebook*'s displacement, its undermining of realist codes, helped to make it in some sort its readers' property. What they found in it was a demonstration that a habit of continuity had been broken – that here the *woman* writer was no longer acting as the mediator of, as Raymond Williams put it, 'a particular apprehension of a relation between individuals and society' (George Eliot had been his major example). Instead Lessing had exposed the business of sustaining characters in their social roles – in 'Free Women' – as papering over the cracks, and allowed the 'real' man, the 'real' woman, to fall apart in the notebooks. She had, of course, clung to the paradox that their mutual disintegration was (still) a form of unity; but her readers deconstructed this paradox on their own initiative. In her Preface to the novel, ten years on, she complained (as she had earlier in interviews):

> nobody so much as noticed this central theme [breakdown], because the book was instantly belittled, by friendly review-ers as well as by hostile ones, as being about the sex war, or was claimed by women as a useful weapon in the sex war.[20]

She *had* worried about being labelled an 'African' novelist – indeed, had passed that worry on to Anna: 'We read novels for information about areas of life we don't know – Nigeria, South Africa. . . . The novel has become a function of the fragmented society, the fragmented consciousness' (*GN*, pp. 67–8). To find herself typecast as a reporter from the dark continent of women exasperated her. However, this was not, as things turned out, a matter of 'information' merely, nor of her having failed to read the signs of the birth of a new feminism – though she undoubtedly hadn't seen them, any more than (as she has Anna point out in the novel) the Rhodesian communist group had seen the signs of emergent black nationalism. What *The Golden Notebook* heralded was a time (our time) of decentring, decolonizing, in all kinds of directions. In this, precisely, lay its timeliness, though it's small wonder Lessing felt oddly dispossessed by its success. She had wanted to see 'breakdown', 'fragmentation', as somehow transitional, *en route* to a newly impersonal, post-personal psychic economy ('growing up is after all only the understanding that one's unique and incredible experience is what everyone shares,' she wrote in her Preface). But the novel's reception implied that the 'histories' – the stories – that lay in wait undereath the realist structure she'd jettisoned were far too divergent and contradictory to be contained in a new version of 'wholeness', however tentative or paradoxical.

Her novel went on deconstructing and reconstructing itself in the world at large – often, ironically enough, into new realist fictions, versions of 'Free Women' (Marilyn French's glum epic, *The Women's Room*, is a recent example). And this too is revealing. We sometimes talk as if – while admitting that, for example, social history, public history, has turned out to be dismayingly unknowable – the history of literature remains intact; so that after 'modernism' comes 'post-modernism' or whatever. Whereas what characterizes contemporary fiction is less 'movements' of this kind than a splintering and scatter of genres and sub-genres. It's at this level, perhaps, that *The Golden Notebook* ultimately symbolizes its contemporaneity. For Lessing it marked a further stage in the process of depersonalizing, disowning one's voice. Her final, wry remark in that Preface ten years on was that controlling one's meanings was, it seemed, after all not the point: 'the book is alive and potent . . . *only* when its plan and shape and intention are not understood.' And her own *œuvre* since then has itself fragmented: stories and novels (most obviously *The Summer Before the Dark*, 1973) that address themselves to 'real' people, 'real' women; and fictions of inner space that go on searching for kinds of wholeness that transcend personal and sexual identity. The *Zeitgeist* – perhaps because of *The Golden Notebook*'s reception – particularly haunts her (if such an openness to the cross-currents of the time can ever be said to be particular). She has become, in tone and in theme, speculative, unpredictable, a connoisseur of (what are dismissed as) unrealities. Among the women, her role, once so problematic, now begins to establish itself as that of wise woman or witch.

\*

Lessing's return to *Children of Violence* came with *Landlocked* (1965), a return that is oddly sketchy and perfunctory. For, although there are gestures toward continuity with the earlier three novels in the sequence, this part of the narrative – which finds Martha now waiting for Anton's naturalization to come through, so that they can divorce and she can leave for England, and finds her waiting, too, as it turns out, for her father's death – is set in a strange limbo. Indeed, *Landlocked* is hardly a narrative at all, and most of its 'events' are not new to the story. Martha feels 'her old enemy, the hound Repetition, snapping at her heels' (*L*, p. 140); and so does the reader: 'Betty Kreiger, Marie du Preez, Marjorie Black. . . . they watched their own deterioration like merciless onlookers. . . . hypnotized into futility by self-observation' (*L*, p. 212). Mrs Van 'sat pleating her blue silk skirt with one fat ringed hand' (*L*, p. 214); in the new younger 'socialist' group 'the dramatis personae were the same, presumably the plot was also' (*L*, p. 282). But this stasis is not just a thematic matter, a display of Martha in waiting. The plot about 'growing up' has itself been recast, so that it is no longer a question of moving on, or achieving one's own identity. *Landlocked* takes up, shorthand-fashion, images and conclusions from *The Golden Notebook*. Martha imagines her life in 'rooms', separate compartments; we are told that her love-affair with the Middle European Jewish settler Thomas Stern (a heroic, but sketchy, figure) unifies her ('From this centre she now lived'; *L*, p. 103), but this blissful stage is abbreviated (shades of Ella and Paul) to make way for the realization that it is in their shared 'sickness' that they're really together (shades of Anna and Saul):

> The soul of the human race, that part of the mind which has no name, is not called Thomas and Martha, which holds the human race as frogspawn is held in jelly – that part of Martha and of Thomas was twisted and warped, was part of a twist and a damage. She could no more disassociate herself from the violence done her than a tadpole can live out of water. (*L*, p. 202)

In short, though the novel keeps up a conventional appearance, it is haunted by an almost savage impatience for a different vision. Martha's father's death, Thomas's death, happen in a casual aside; Mrs Quest, seen up to now only through Martha's eyes, comes suddenly – for a brief, vivid interlude – into focus, dreaming of her own mother, and trapped in a world of sickness with her dying husband. But perhaps the clearest sign that this is a book that resents its own form is Thomas's legacy: the crazy, fragmentary manuscript which is the fruit of his self-imposed vigil with a doomed tribe in the bush, and which Martha takes with her, on an impulse, into exile. It's a version, she suggests, of 'anthropology' (*L*, p. 280); done, not by an 'objective' observer, but by a crazed and haunted man who speaks in the voices of a dozen conflicting personalities – despairing, saintly, scabrous, derisive ... Echoes, again, of *The Golden Notebook*, and a foretaste of *The Four-Gated City*, whose form is, as Lessing put it, 'shot to hell'.[21]

In *The Four-Gated City* (1969), the fifth book of the sequence, her twenty years of living in England spill out in one monstrous chronicle. More: the appendixed scenario (notes up to the year 2000) produces a span that violently alters the pace and scope of *Children of Violence*. Lessing was rewriting her series from the end, and in a brief afterword she suggested a collective name for it: a *Bildungsroman*, an educational and utopian fiction. As Dagmar Barnouw observes, it is only *The Four-Gated City* that justifies the use of such a label without irony.[22] Here Martha achieves the destiny which (we are now meant to see) was somehow lurking unrecognized in her inconclusiveness and muddle. And, to this end, Lessing recalls and reworks her heroine's moments of 'illumination'. Newly arrived Martha, wandering London streets, still a euphoric and exhausted traveller, returns to her beginnings: 'a young girl sitting under the tree. . . . nothing to do with Martha, or any other name she might have had attached to her' (*FGC*, p. 48), on the brink of a 'new place' in her consciousness. And though her visions solidify in a (true) picture of her London future – 'a large layered house . . . full of . . . half-grown people . . . herself, a middle-aged woman' (*FGC*, p. 73) – this time it is not a refuge to 'live inside'.

Her role in Mark Coldridge's household (secretary, house-keeper, substitute wife, surrogate mother) seems almost ludicrously remote from her idea of herself. But in fact Mark, his sick wife Lynda and the more or less lost children who make up the 'family' expose her to what is most disturbing in the culture. In them, the rationalist, progressive, secular assumptions that have underpinned an ideal Englishness – and indeed, we're meant to understand, Martha's communist idealism – are brought to a destructive test. Numinous 'underground' notions take root and flourish among the ruins of the old liberalism. They are not, however, merely *observed* as signs of the times: 'the narrator Lessing withdraws from the tone of omniscience, from explanations, comparisons, encouragement, and patient irony'.[23] A deliberately crude – but still crude – collective consciousness invades the narrative, unmediated by the fiction of a personal destiny.

To put it another way, this is a novel of the 1960s. Lessing seems to have found herself finally 'at home' in England in these years, because now the culture itself was taking on a vagrant, apocalyptic tone. In this new gnosticism she read signs of a historical transformation – a mutation almost – that showed people were internalizing and (just possibly) trickily transcending their violent heritage. The grasping after 'wholeness' she'd traced so ironically in Martha's relations with the sports club or the communist group now seemed to have acquired a saving impersonality. The old utopian dream of the city, for instance, lives in Mark's imagination just as vividly as in Martha's; Lynda's officially diagnosed 'schizophrenia' is a matter of 'plugging in' to a 'wavelength' that has always broadcast the news from nowhere. The crassness of the metaphors (plugging in, and so on) announces that this is a narrative that has done with decorum, verbal or otherwise:

> [society] is like one of those sea creatures who have tentacles or arms equipped with numbing poisons: anything new, whether hostile or helpful, must be stunned into immobility. . . . The process is accomplished, in this society, through words. . . . communism, traitor, espionage, homosexuality, teenage violence. . . . Or anger, or commitment, or satire. . . . Anarchy, irresponsibility, decadence, selfishness – into this box, behind this label, gets put every kind of behaviour by which the creature is made nervous. . . . quick, quick, a new word, a new label, 'commitment', perhaps? 'mysticism?' (FGC, pp. 465–6)

Sardonic mock-analyses like this abound. In this one Lessing defiantly signposts her own dubious progress (communism to 'mysticism?') while at the same time disowning all such labels. Her new intellectual allies – R. D. Laing, Sufi mystics – are, she's aware, almost bywords for fashionable unreason. But that fact, on her logic, convicts the culture that 'names' them.

There are thus at least two main kinds of cultural 'story' in *The Four-Gated City*: the public, realistic one which pretends to continuity (but actually rests on amnesia) and the underground one which is structured by apocalypse. This sounds like

61

the curious format of the first *Children of Violence* novels over again (see pp. 32–5 above), but the crucial difference now is that it's the future that's shaping the present. Clairvoyance, not memory, provides the narrative 'time bombs', and as a result time lays itself out topographically. The important moves are *lateral*. One minor illustration of this is the question of Martha's age. In the opening pages she's the age she's supposed to be (thirty-ish), but as soon as she joins the Coldridge household she becomes unreasonably middle-aged, so that it's a struggle to remind oneself her life isn't mostly over. And of course in a sense it is: she (and we) have entered the future-haunted territory of Anna's/Saul's Golden Notebook or Thomas's anthropological collage from *Landlocked*, where the knowledge of death and decay is ever-present, and where the 'personal' (represented here by the rejected role of likeable 'Matty') disperses itself. Another way of putting this is that characters no longer stand independently in the mid-space between author and reader: Martha becomes her author's age.

London is from the start an imagined city – most poignantly so for working-class Iris, Martha's first friend and protector (compare Rose in *In Pursuit of the English*):

> Put her brain, together with the other million brains, women's brains, that recorded in such tiny loving anxious detail the histories of windowsills, skins of paint, replaced curtains and salvaged baulks of timber, there would be a recording instrument, a sort of six-dimensional map which included the histories and lives and loves of people, London – a section map in depth. (*FGC*, p. 20)

This 'loving anxious' consciousness tries to assert continuity across the blitz and the bomb sites, and fails. Women have been the curators of the fabric of society, and still play the part (Martha's role in the Coldridge household), but now it is merely a 'holding operation', for this whole way of life is being 'depth-charged' from somewhere else. The shorthand for what happens is '1956':

the laws which operate have in fact nothing at all to do with
. . . the way of thinking that gives 1956 five stars for importance, except that perhaps it is, just here, that we pay tribute
to the other pattern, momentarily visible.

> Subtract the words Suez, Hungary, with their associations
> of communism, revisionism, imperialism, etc. etc., what
> there is left is . . . that a great many people, in one way or
> another, said: No, enough, no more of that. And they milled
> about in open places in this city and that . . . (*FGC*, p. 303)

In pursuit of 'the other pattern', Lessing describes the rebuild-
ing of London, in an extraordinary passage, as a continuous
explosion:

> London heaved up and down, houses changed shape, col-
> lapsed, whole streets were vanishing into rubble, and arrow
> shapes in cement reached up into the clouds. . . . If time were
> slightly speeded up, then a city now must look like fountains
> of rubble cascading among great machines, while buildings
> momentarily form, change colour like vegetation, dissolve,
> reform. (*FGC*, pp. 314–15)

This galvanic city – the London of the 1960s – gives the lie to
notions of continuity, 'as if the idea of a city or town as
something slow-changing, almost permanent, belonged to the
past' (*FGC*, pp. 314–15). It lives in a euphoric state of change,
an orgy of mobility. And yet, Lessing pushes us to see, its
changefulness has two faces. One is personified in Mark's
mother, Margaret Patten, a grand-scale hostess, and an exact
barometer of trends and tones and tendencies. Her surname
says as much; Lessing indeed seems to have married her to her
1960s husband, a homosexual, to make the point. Margaret's
parties enact the pattern of repressive tolerance, repressive
naming and labelling, which masks real change, 'the other
pattern'. That, Lessing wants to say, is one of radical disintegration – in the culture, and in the individual, where it shows
itself as (what's labelled as) madness.

Mark's wife Lynda, who has long given up playing wife to

him, or mother to their son, and who has been diagnosed as a sick, regressive inadequate, is the key to the codes of change. Barbara Rigney points out Lessing's closeness here to R. D. Laing's 'anti-psychiatry'; also, that she is deliberately transforming an old female nightmare about madness: 'As Bronte's Bertha can be seen as Jane Eyre's mad, bad self, so Lynda can be seen as Martha's mad, good self'. Lynda lives in the basement, 'a location perhaps more appropriate as a symbolic hell than the attic room in which Bertha is confined'.[24] The basement is also (compare the story 'The Other Woman') a reminder of wartime, and a fitting refuge for the unconscious in its protest against the craziness of the explosive city. Lynda's marriage to Mark is frankly offered as a paradigm of a compartmentalized world: she untouchable and self-imprisoned in the cellarage, he the rational, decent, objective man, turning his study upstairs into one terrible worldwide wall-chart of famine, pollution, war and doomsday weapons. Martha, moving between them, proceeds unmistakably from Mark's world to Lynda's. He belongs to the past, with his utopian novel *A City in the Desert*, and his love-affair with communism. Lynda belongs there too, one might think – given *The Golden Notebook*'s exploration of breakdown. But here madness is not a matter merely of dissolving the boundaries between selves: 'it is not a question of "Lynda's mind" or "Martha's mind"; it is the human mind, or part of it' (*FGC*, p. 513). What madness reveals is the existence of a dark continent that has been falsely mapped and whited out (most recently by psychiatry); and what emerges from the basement is a counter-culture, the stuff of gothic and of science fiction.

In other words, it is an area of fiction that has been cordoned off precisely because it allows that there are more things in heaven and earth than are dreamt of in (even) liberal Mark's philosophy. We encounter our fears, our futures, only in fiction we don't respect. Lessing works this one through in the character of Jimmy Woods, Mark's business partner, who writes science fiction in his spare time while actually (unknown to Mark) working on advanced techniques for the military use of telepathy, brainwashing, and so on. Jimmy, who is, Lessing suggests, little better than a robot intelligence himself, and who is certainly a more or less allegorical character, represents the (paranoid) possibility that, while the reasonable people (Mark) recoil from the messy, squalid, embarrassing 'occult', the powers that be will take it over. The main enemy, however, is common sense itself: the shared, realist perspective that places people in the middle distance and (as it were) takes humanity for granted. What happens when you discard that perspective is graphically illustrated in Martha's vision of the crowds in Oxford Street:

> There they were, all soft like pale slugs, or dark slugs, with their limp flabby flesh, with hair sprouting from it, and the things like hooves on their feet. . . . with their roundish bony heads, that had flaps of flesh sticking out on either side, then the protruberance in the middle, with the air vents in it, and the eyes, tinted-jelly eyes which had a swivelling movement that gave them a life of their own . . . they all looked half-drugged or half-asleep, dull, as if the creatures had been hypnotized or poisoned. For these people walked in their fouled and disgusting streets full of ordure and bits of refuse and paper as if they were not conscious of their existence here . . . (*FGC*, p. 521)

To see 'them, us, the human race' from this alien viewpoint, 'as visitors from a space ship might see them' (*FGC*, p. 521) – or as mad Lynda has long seen them – is to lose your inhibitions about radically alternative views of 'progress'.

Martha assembles a new reading list:

> books on Rosicrucianism and the old Alchemists; Buddhist books . . . Yoga . . . Zoroastrianism and esoteric Christianity . . . the I Ching; Zen, witchcraft, magic, astrology and vampirism; scholarly treatises on Sufism; the works of the Christian mystics. . . . everything rejected by official culture and scholarship. (*FGC*, p. 528)

And *The Four-Gated City* takes off into a blueprint for the future. The disasters that overtake 'civilization' are those foreseen in Mark's wall-charts, but the means of survival are supplied from the areas of the psyche mapped by Lynda and Martha: prevision (exodus from the cities), telepathy (communication outside the war machine), a vision of the world as one organism. A new generation of children is born knowing the worst ('they are beings who include that history in themselves and who have transcended it'; *FGC*, p. 662) and so able to imagine the better. The centres of life are in Mongolia, or Africa, and the novel's fragmentary dispatches from the future end with a memo on a mutant black child, Joseph, whose job will be 'to inspect parks and gardens' in a new city once called Nairobi.

In bringing *Children of Violence* full circle this way, Lessing imposes a certain level of coherence, and at the same time exposes its essential discontinuity. Her series has folded over on itself, on the pivot of the novel that stepped aside, *The Golden Notebook*, so that now 'exile' turns out to mean a very literal, extraterrestrial kind of alienation, surveying experience as if from outer (actually from inner) space. Looking back, one can make connections: the adolescent Martha's intuition that 'What was demanded of her was that she should accept something quite different' (*MQ*, p. 62) now reads like a most prophetic insight. But it was not. What these words looked forward to as Lessing wrote them (in 1952) was almost certainly the communist idealism she recorded ironically (in *A Ripple from the Storm*) in 1958, when she had herself left the Party. This is a laborious way of making an obvious point: that *Children of Violence* not only describes a crisis in progressive thinking but is itself an exemplary casualty – a deliberate disaster area. When Lessing writes about the feel and texture of life in the later pages of *The Four-Gated City*, it is to make a parodic joke – as when she describes Lynda and Martha putting themselves together to face the world after a session in the basement:

Lynda's hair, in a graceful chignon, was coloured strawberry-roan. Her eyes, enormous now, were enhanced by silver, jade-green, ash-grey salves. Her make-up made the most of the prominent facial bones of her skull. . . . Martha's hair was light brown, cut . . . in a short glossy helmet shape. A look of health had always, she felt, suited her; and her face was tinted a very faint rose with a hint of apricot. (*FGC*, pp. 540–1)

This is a portrait of two space travellers disguising themselves to join humanity, and the tone includes a savage sneer at humanity's expense (so easily taken in). Mark is allowed a final protest on behalf of common sense – 'I can't stand that nasty mixture of irony and St John of the Cross and the Arabian Nights they all . . . went in for' (*FGC*, p. 667) – but then his main role is to let us know that Lessing knows precisely what she's doing.

In a 1969 interview she measured something of her distance from the writer who had claimed that one could speak for others in 'a small personal voice':

Since writing *The Golden Notebook* I've become less personal. I've floated away from the personal. I've stopped saying, 'This is *mine*, this is *my* experience'. . . . I don't believe any more that I have a thought. There is a thought around.[25]

*The Four-Gated City* is – designedly, though it seems paradoxical to say so – a collage, an anthology, an offering to the spirit of the age. Not only has Martha the person disintegrated, but so has the author as person, and as a result the form is indeed 'shot to hell'. Lynn Sukenick emphasizes Lessing's 'deliberateness in dreaming, this encouragement of the unconscious to serve conscious, problematic purpose'.[26] However, while Lessing is convincing on her alienation from the realist perspective, she hasn't yet found a way of giving her 'other pattern' – inner space – much depth or force. Sometimes she seems to be writing as though her audience either knows all about it already, or never will: as though – in the oldest of mystic paradoxes – there are no words, only more or less obstructive, or more or less handy, labels.

*

Her next two novels, *Briefing for a Descent into Hell* (1971) and *The Summer Before the Dark* (1973), both confirm the suspicion that, having turned her style and her way of thinking inside out, Lessing had for the moment depleted her resources as a writer. Whatever her convictions on the matter, the territory of speculative fiction was new to her; and she explored it, to begin with, without subtlety. On the other hand, she no longer wrote like a realist exactly, either. Thus while these two novels are very different – *Briefing*, inner space fiction; *Summer*, the 'story' of Kate Brown's awakening to middle age – each of them gives off a sense of incompleteness and thinness. This is connected, of course, with their themes – or, rather, theme, which is the grotesque and cramping inadequacy of the 'identities' people find themselves saddled with in mid-life. But it's also a matter of guttering energy. *Briefing for a Descent into Hell*, in particular, suffers from the difficulty of making the old mythic and metaphysical landmarks new. Its nameless protagonist has escaped from his life as Charles Watkins, Professor of Classics, to embark on his own odyssey in the unconscious. Many of the images are tired or token ones: Plato and Campanella and generations in between and since have described this city; Sinbad, Gulliver, the Ancient Mariner, Hardy's Dynasts and Doomsters have been this way before. Yet the narrative doesn't acknowledge the fact, except perhaps by its impatience, its offering of tokens *as* tokens. The most urgent and self-conscious writing (though this section too picks up an old dream of Anna's in *The Golden Notebook*, pp. 293–4) is concerned to create an overview of the earth as a web of colour and light, sustained by cosmic balances. Here, vocations attain a Neoplatonic Form ('not soldiers, but Soldier, not artists, but Artist'; *BDH*, p. 95), and nations have a being as natural as seas or deserts:

I had an old thought, or rather, an old thought was trans-

68

planted upwards into the keener, swifter air of this realm, that no matter what changes of government or what names were given to a nation's system of organization, there was always the same flavour or reality that remained in that place . . . (*BDH*, p. 98)

No 'flavour or reality', however, adheres to individuals, and professors seem to have lost their place in the scheme of things and to be dedicated to tranquillizing real (impersonal) memory, just like the wretched doctors who will restore Professor Charles Watkins to his prison of sanity.

The 'I' of *Briefing for a Descent into Hell* is dedicated to the death of the 'I':

To celestial eyes, seen like a broth of microbes under a microscope . . . this scum of microbes . . . begins slowly to sense itself as one, a function, a note in the harmony, and this *is* its point and function . . . and never where these mad microbes say I, I, I, I, I, for saying I, I, I, I, is their madness. . . . What sent us off centre, and away from the sweet sanity of We? (*BDH*, pp. 102–3)

This passage, of course, also recalls many earlier ones: most surprisingly, perhaps, the ending of the African novella 'Hunger' almost twenty years before:

in the tribe and the kraal, the life of his fathers had been built on the word *we*. . . . And between then and now has been a harsh and ugly time when there was only the word I, I, I – as cruel and sharp as a knife. (*CAS* 2, p. 330)

There, according to her own later account, Lessing had been straining towards a language of collectivity she couldn't really produce, and the same seems true of *Briefing for a Descent into Hell*. Indeed, the earlier Marxist fable is rather less thin, less schematic, than the later novel.

'Woman' is not one of the vocations visible to 'celestial eyes' in *Briefing for a Descent into Hell*, nor is 'wife', nor is 'mother'; and it is on this point that *The Summer Before the Dark* turns.

In a way it is a 'woman's book', an offering possibly to the readers who felt cheated by Martha's dissolution, and unconvinced of the tenuousness of sexual identity.[27] Kate Brown's panic when she finds herself redundant at 45 (children grown, a bland marital *détente*) is described in the idiom of the current feminist novel (partly created, since 1962, out of *The Golden Notebook*):

> Patience. Self-discipline. Self-control. Self-abnegation. Chastity. Adaptability to others – this above all. . . . She could remember very clearly the day when, reading certain words that seemed old-fashioned, in an old novel, she had thought: Well, that's what *this* is. . . . Looking back . . . it seemed to her that she had acquired not virtues but a form of dementia. (*SBD*, p. 89)

Kate finds herself doing exactly what magazines' agony aunts would recommend: glamorous new job, clothes, hairdo; travel, a new man, and so on. But this cheery prescription doesn't work. The job and the image are variants of what she's sick of, what she's been doing for years; and when first the man, and then she, fall literally sick in Spain she understands it as a sign that she must return to England (but not *home*), and take time to be alone and to think.

It's here that her story starts to overlap with *Briefing*'s inner odyssey, and with Martha's and Lynda's self-experiments in *The Four-Gated City*. She stares appalled, on the street, in the theatre (she has seen that it's something about role-playing):

> people, animals rather, all looking in one direction, at other dressed-up animals lifted up to perform on a stage, animals covered with cloth and bits of fur, ornamented with stones, their faces and claws painted with colour. Everyone had just finished eating animal of some kind; and the furs . . . were from animals that had lived and played and fornicated in forests and fields . . . and their hair . . . mats and caps and manes and wigs of hair . . . (*SBD*, p. 149)

Kate, who has always loved her red hair, lets it grow now into a

grey bush, and sees herself as a 'sick monkey'; she also per-
severes with a serial dream, in which she labours across a
winter landscape to carry a stranded seal to the sea. In short,
she understands herself to be an animal among animals; sees
herself with something like 'celestial eyes', and her sexuality,
from this viewpoint, as a banal – if 'natural' – confidence trick:

> A goose just out of its egg follows a shape . . . and is
> imprinted ever after by 'Mother'. . . . A woman walking in a
> sagging dress, with a heavy walk, and her hair . . . not
> conforming to the prints made by fashions, is not 'set' to
> attract. . . . The same woman in a dress cut in this or that
> way . . . and click. . . . Men's attention is stimulated by
> signals no more complicated than what leads the gosling . . .
> (SBD, pp. 176–7)

Again, the writing wears thin. Kate becomes a modest
woman's Martha, freed into 'greyness', cured of personality.

The issues surrounding personality and character dominate
during these years (the 1960s and the early 1970s) – Lessing's
perception of herself in the character of writer most particularly. She moved away from realism (and from communism)
towards fantasy and science fiction, and, though this may
sound like a 'development', *The Golden Notebook* and *The
Four-Gated City* reveal how traumatic it was, a period of
imaginative schizophrenia. She was becoming, one might say, a
psychic communist, but to do that she had turned herself inside
out, 'turned her mind around', as the mystics always painfully
put it. If she began in England as an exile, after twenty-odd
years she was an alien. The 'English' stories collected in *A Man
and Two Women* (1963) and *The Story of a Non-Marrying
Man* (1972) are altogether more variegated and uncertain than
the African pieces. Some treat the incursions of the unreal
realistically: 'The Temptation of Jack Orkeney', for instance,
looks at the 'occult' question in the context of an old socialist's
shame at 'getting religion'; 'To Room Nineteen' is a suicidal
variant on *The Summer Before the Dark*. 'Report on the
Threatened City', on the other hand, takes off in a spaceship

with some intergalactic welfare workers to document a patho-
logically complacent species.

Perhaps the most interesting stories – hardly stories, rather
studies – are those that picture the gradual, seasonal life of
parks and gardens: 'A Year in Regent's Park', 'Lions, Leaves,
Roses . . .', 'The Other Garden'. Here, for long moments,
London seems what it so signally failed to be for her – the ideal
city where human change and natural change might meld:
'Leaves, words, people, shadows, whirled together towards
autumn and solstice' (*CS* 2, p. 182). The most telling images,
though, are those of violence past, present and future: the
ancient 'gypsy' Hetty in 'An Old Woman and Her Cat', on the
run from the social workers and the Home, finding a refuge in a
developers' paradise in 'amiable Hampstead':

> There was no glass left anywhere. The flooring was mostly
> gone, leaving small platforms and juts of planking over
> basements full of water. The ceilings were crumbling. The
> roofs were going. The houses were like bombed buildings.
> (*CS* 2, p. 169)

# 3

## NEW WORLDS

*The Memoirs of a Survivor* (1974) does not step over into speculative fiction any more decisively than *Briefing for a Descent into Hell* or *The Four-Gated City*, but it does locate the *threshold* between Lessing's worlds a lot more persuasively. Here, her shift in ideas is a shift in perception: the narrative has an illusionist, teasing quality that questions the 'real' with a new expertise. It is, in several ways, and for all its brevity, a stock-taking book. She described it, on the dustjacket, as 'an attempt at autobiography', doubtless because it reconnects her with some of her oldest material (the family scenario, for instance); but it also takes stock of certain of her resources as a writer, and in this its function resembles that of *The Golden Notebook* – very distantly, of course, since now a great deal (about role-playing, about inner space) is taken for granted. And she is not, this time, precipitating a crisis, but rather mulling over what turns out to have happened to her. Her tone is calm, almost elegiac: she's writing from the other side of the mirror, as it were, chronicling the processes of dissolution with a lucid patience that is itself shocking, almost witty.

*The Memoirs of a Survivor* begins with the death of a city – a London that has lost its name, where warmth, food, water and even oxygen drain away, until, gradually, people are left living off the corpse, scavenging, stealing, bartering. It is a picture that recalls other versions of 'last days' (the pigsties and garden plots that invaded ancient Rome, for instance), but the writing stresses to the end the eerie persistence of a sense of normality: 'While everything, all forms of social organization, broke up, we lived on, adjusting our lives, as if nothing fundamental was happening' (*MS*, p. 19). Breaches in 'outside' reality are quickly matched in private perceptions: the narrator, semi-besieged in her solid, ground-floor flat, turns from watching the new 'tribes' gather on the pavement, to find the blank wall of her room dissolving into other rooms, other times. And still the sense of matter-of-factness persists. When a complete stranger materializes in her living room, to make her the custodian of 12-year-old Emily, the 'impossible' situation must be accepted (as if it were some kind of administrative mistake) because otherwise nothing can be trusted. So life goes on – the narrator stepping now, almost routinely, through the wall into other spaces; Emily, hungry for life, joining the tribes of the pavement, losing her identity before she achieves it:

> any individual consummations were nothing beside this act of mingling constantly with others, as if some giant rite of eating were taking place, everyone tasting and licking and regurgitating everyone else, making themselves known to others and others known to them in this tasting and sampling – eyeing each other, rubbing shoulders and bodies, talking, exchanging emanations. (*MS*, p. 74)

As the boundaries dissolve, it seems at first that the inner space must be a refuge, a liberation to counter this repulsiveness, but no: the experience is more anomalous than that.

For example: people seem to be turning into animals (herding, migrating), but what is it to be 'animal'? One of the novel's most quietly bizarre effects is to invent (along with Emily) an 'impossible' creature, Hugo, a cat-dog, or dog-cat, who has all the conviction (but none of the merely whimsical appeal) of an animal in a fairy tale. Since the narrative accepts Hugo's presence with only a momentary grinding of gears, and since he's several times in danger of being eaten, we accept him too, perforce, as yet another anomaly. And one contradictory image serves to support another, so that it is with little surprise that we realize that the realm behind the wall 'belongs' to both Emily and the narrator – a composite childhood. Here the 'personal' life that is so under threat in the outside world is traced to its family origins, and inner space proves problematic in its turn. In fragmentary scenes from the nursery, the drawing room, the bedroom, a small girl is formed into a person: made to know her separateness, her nuisance value, her mother's resentment and weariness, her father's furtive sexuality. These ghosts are horribly solid: 'tall, large, with a clean-china healthiness, all blue eyes, pink cheeks, and the jolly no-nonsense mouth of a schoolgirl' (*MS*, p. 59); 'a soldier. . . . conventionally handsome face . . . half-hidden by a large moustache' (*MS*, p. 60). They recall Mr and Mrs Quest, and, beyond them, Lessing's images of her own parents. They are 'characters', and they manufacture a character – a rebellious, guilty girl, self-repressed in her mother's image.

The climactic scene on this inner stage (where everything is gigantized by a child's perspective) traces 'character-forming' back to the denial of the animal, and the denial of hunger:

Emily, absorbed, oblivious. She was eating – chocolate. No, excrement. . . . She had smeared it on sheets and blankets . . . over her face and into her hair, and there she sat, a little monkey, thoughtfully tasting and digesting. (*MS*, p. 123)

The traumatic cleansing that follows ('naughty, disgusting, filthy, dirty, dirty, dirty'; *MS*, p. 124) leaves an indelible sobbing on the air. And, when the narrator next enters this realm, she tracks that down too:

The finding had about it, had in it as its quintessence, the banality, the tedium, the smallness, the restriction, of that 'personal' dimension. What else could I find – unexpectedly, it goes without saying . . . a blonde, blue-eyed child . . . reddened and sullen with weeping. Who else could it possibly be but Emily's mother, the large carthorse woman, her tormentor, the world's image? (*MS*, p. 128)

Infinite regress. . . Each generation has stamped its own

discipline, its own wretchedly acquired boundaries, on the next. The 'personal' is not the unique: its claustrophobia derives precisely from its repetitions.

This replay of the family scenario clears the stage, little by little. Intercut with the character-acting, and with the increasingly anarchic glimpses of the dying city outside, are visions of the inner space depopulated, exorcized – moving pictures that take up and transform the imagery of destruction:

> walking through a light screen of leaves, flowers, birds, blossom, the essence of woodland brought to life in the effaced patterns of the wallpaper, I moved through rooms that seemed to have aged since I saw them last. The walls had thinned, had lost substance to the air, to time; everywhere on the forest floor stood slight tall walls, all upright still and in their proper pattern of angles, but ghosts of walls, like the flats in a theatre. (*MS*, p. 86)

Again (this is almost the determining flavour of *Memoirs*) echoes from earlier works open out/close down into mystery, anomaly: here, echoes of Lessing's blitzed London ('shock after shock . . . through brick and plaster') from *In Pursuit of the English*; or the stage direction from her 1958 *Play with a Tiger*, where the walls vanish to show the actors against the backdrop of the city; or the scene in the basement in *The Four-Gated City* where Lynda pushes at the walls with her scarified fingers. For not the least of the illusionist effects in *Memoirs* is the gradual identification of the emptying city with the emptying inner space – so that the new barbarism without is overwritten by the transcendence of the 'personal' within. In its final move, the novel crumples up its world like a sheet of paper:

> that world, presenting itself in a thousand little flashes, a jumble of little scenes, facets of another picture, all impermanent, was folding up as we stepped into it, was parcelling itself up, was vanishing, dwindling and going – all of it, trees and streams, grasses and rooms and people. (*MS*, p. 182)

Into this vortex the narrator, Hugo (naturally), Emily, her shapeless man and a horde of gutter-children cram themselves, to meet an unimaginable future.

It is a version of space travel without the trappings. Or almost: in this last scene there is a fleeting apparition – 'I only saw her for a moment, in a time like the fading of a spark on dark air' (*MS*, p. 182) – of a tutelary being (a cosmic mother) from the 'other' side. This enigmatic figure was, as it turns out, a clue to where Lessing was bound next – her future Muse. *The Memoirs of a Survivor* might have suggested a sojourn in self-consciousness, the kind of retrospective transformation of earlier works that characterized, say, late Nabokov (*Transparent Things, Look at the Harlequins*). But Lessing was not a writer to identify (she would probably say, confuse) the inner space of art – reflexiveness, self-anatomy – with the space in consciousness she was interested in. She stepped out of the mirror-world of metafiction with her wanderlust and her epic ambitions unscathed: this time, as a fully paid-up alien, into the outer space of a new series, *Canopus in Argos: Archives*, which consists to date of four novels – *Re: Colonized Planet 5, Shikasta* (1979), *The Marriages Between Zones Three, Four, and Five* (1980), *The Sirian Experiments* (1981) and *The Making of the Representative for Planet 8* (1982).

*

*Shikasta* was started in the belief that it would be a single self-contained book, and that when it was finished I would be done with the subject. But as I wrote I was invaded with ideas for other books, other stories, and the exhilaration that comes from being set free into a larger scope, with more capacious possibilities and themes. It was clear that I had made – or found – a new world for myself, a realm where the petty fates of planets, let alone individuals, are only aspects of cosmic evolution expressed in the rivalries and inter-actions of great galactic Empires . . . (*S*, 'Some Remarks', p. ix)

This sounds more like the territory of a Kurt Vonnegut than a Nabokov – though one mischievous parenthetical reference in *Shikasta* to '(Marcel Proust, sociologist and anthropologist)' (*S*, p. 158) suggests that in the long view we may be surprised to find how much of the art we think of as produced in ivory towers (or cork-lined studies) turns out to be useful. Science-fiction writers 'have played the . . . role of the despised illegitimate son who can afford to tell truths the respectable siblings . . . do not dare' (*S*, p. x).

Lessing's euphoria is clearly fuelled by joining the ranks of the unrespectable – but more than that: for the first time since the early novels of *Children of Violence* she is writing inside a genre. Admittedly a genre that can stomach nearly anything (compare Mark's line in *The Four-Gated City* about 'that nasty mixture of irony and St John of the Cross and the Arabian Nights') but, still, a containing fiction in which her anomalous points of view, divergent time-scales and characters from animals to angels can coexist without continuous tension. Space fiction is not only realism's bastard offspring, but harks back to earlier ages of storytelling – romance, for instance, in the 'sword and sorcery' division; and, more broadly, the happy pre-novel formulas, like those of the *Decameron* or *The Canterbury Tales*, which haven't yet discovered the single point of view.

This, though, is to make *Shikasta* sound a lot more cheerful than it is. Lessing's tone in her prefatory 'Remarks' had, perhaps, more to do with *The Marriages Between Zones Three, Four and Five*, which was, she implies, already finished and waiting in the wings. *Shikasta* is about human history as an episode in cosmic 'time', and much of it focuses on the wretched present and near-future (last days, as in *The Four-Gated City*), documenting our slide into pollution, starvation and near-extinction, with Youth Armies roaming a Europe threatened with genocide by the Third World (our terminology). The only sense in which, here, Lessing has found a 'new world' is that she has discovered a point of view that wrenches her out of the orbit of emotional commitment – the long, long view of the cosmic archivists, who record and collate these horrors with a cool, dispassionate eye, and for whom the end is never the end.

'Shikasta' (Earth) is colonized in its infancy by three galactic empires: technological Sirius, which operates in the southern hemisphere, and believes in removing all traces of its experiments (but fails to); vampiric Shammat, which feeds on pain (that is, most of history); and benevolent, mysterious Canopus, which helped form humanity in the beginning, has watched over it since, and now awaits – and 'influences' – the end of history, and the survival of the species. All along, angels were Canopean agents trying to mitigate the effects of the Fall, the planetary dis-aster which left men star-crossed, unable to attune their stone transmitters or build their geometrical cities right. History is a by-product of cosmography: 'We are all creatures of the stars and their forces, they make us, we make them, we are part of a dance from which we by no means and not ever may consider ourselves separate' (S, p. 40). When religions told us we had a 'soul', they were distortedly echoing a Canopean instruction to retain always our 'substance-of-we-feeling', SOWF.

Lessing's main narrator, Johor, a reluctant Canopean expert in Shikastan affairs, does, however, generate ambiguities. Is he, perhaps, affected by the crazed atmosphere of the planet? Or is it that Lessing cannot quite, in her anger against anger, maintain the archivist's cool? At any event, she settles old scores – with the tyranny of ideology, with the criminal indifference of, very specifically, British governments to events in Africa, and so on. Another voice from the past is Lynda Coldridge's, reminding us that we usually perceive only '5 per cent' of the whole (S, p. 183), and providing a punishing, satiric perspective on our greeds and desires: 'Love love love love love. If I had liked it when he slobbered all over me and stuck his hands and things into me then that would have meant I loved him I suppose' (S, p. 186). We are all much sicker than Lynda: 'To identify with ourselves as individuals – this is the very essence of the Degenerative Disease' (S, p. 38). People of the last days

79

learn to contemplate their own individual extinction:

> Nothing they handle or see has substance, and so they repose in their imaginations on chaos, making strength from the possibilities of a creative destruction. They are weaned from everything but the knowledge that the universe is a roaring engine of creativity, and that they are only temporary manifestations of it. (*S*, p. 203)

In this they are reaching towards the archivists' attitude, and it seems not a bad description of Lessing's own position now. *Shikasta* is dedicated to her father, 'who used to sit . . . outside our house in Africa, watching the stars. "Well," he would say, "if we blow ourselves up, there's plenty more where we came from!"' Time is our disease, space our cure: *Shikasta* ends as it begins with a vision of a world that lives in this awareness, with men breeding and dying as the slow stars dictate, in stone circles, triangles, crescents (crescent people in crescent cities), listening to the clear, minimal signals from across the light years.

*The Marriages Between Zones Three, Four and Five* hastens, seemingly, to assuage a certain charmlessness in this stony harmony. It has a medieval flavour, rather like those paintings and tapestries that simultaneously show you figures – the wise men, perhaps – on each stage of their journey, as if they paused now and then in attitudes that (they knew) would delight the iconographers. Except that here we have wise women: Zone Three is a magical matriarchy, sophisticated, sensual and intuitive (they understand their animals and send messages by tree), whose queen Al·Ith is summoned by the unseen 'Providers' on a mission she hates: to marry Ben Ata, the warrior king of Zone Four – which, of course, is martial, hierarchical, mysogynistic, and so on. This is the region of fable, where roles are richly fulfilled. But that is never enough, which is why Zones Three and Four must mate, to disturb them into aspiration – a degree of alienation, even. Ben Ata certainly needs Al·Ith (his country is poverty-stricken and wretched), though it is not immediately clear why she needs him. The centre of the

80

novel is an elegant, sad comedy of sexual love, as role-playing:

'You like red then?'
'I think I like *you*,' said he, in spite of himself grabbing at her – for he did not, he liked her even less than before . . . he had in fact forgotten the independence of her, which informed every smile, look, gesture.
She evaded him and slid away into the room, with a mocking backward look over her shoulder which quite astounded her – she did not know she had it in her! (*MBZ*, p. 66)

They do contrive to love each other, however, and gradually to see what the Providers had in mind: neither settling down nor synthesis, but an infinite extension of the repertoire of roles. The picturesque protagonists start on new journeys. Al·Ith, no longer at home in her land, looks for the first time to the high frontiers of Zone Two, where there live creatures (fairies, chimeras) a lot more mythic than she; Ben Ata moves to a wilder, more animal existence in Zone Five. 'What are all these guises, aspects, presentations? Only manifestations of *what we all are* at different times' (*MBZ*, p. 197). The voice is that of one of the Chroniclers of Zone Three, a wise hereditary bard, and what he points to is the proper restlessness that afflicts even the most fabulous and harmonious figures of story. Living in harmony with the Providers (always anonymous here, but presumably Canopeans in one of their guises) is to play roles, not to be entrapped by them.

It does seem, though, that there are roles it is better not to play, and moves better not made. There is a caveat about 'movements' in Lessing's account of the somehow disappointing journey of the Zone Four women, newly liberated, to Zone Three. Her men and women are part of a continuum from animals to angels and beyond, and should not spend all their energies playing themselves.[28] In fact, one of the things Lessing likes best about her matriarchy is that they talk with animals, and this is a major theme of the next *Canopus in Argos* novel, *The Sirian Experiments* (1981), where the 'experiments' are in various ways (from hideous games with vivisection to complex questions of colonial responsibility) to do with the human animal. Hugo, the dog-cat from *Memoirs*, seems relevant here:

> I think that all this time, human beings have been watched by creatures whose perceptions and understanding have been so far in advance of anything we have been able to accept, because of our vanity, that we would be appalled if we were able to know, would be humiliated. We have been living with them as blundering, blind, callous, cruel murderers and torturers, and they have watched and known us. (*MS*, pp. 71–2)

Out of context, these animal watchers sound remarkably like Canopean agents, and it would not be surprising to find that in some sense they are.

What *The Sirian Experiments* and the latest novel in the series, *The Making of the Representative for Planet 8* (1982), do make clear is that the central theme of *Canopus in Argos* is species-consciousness – the dialectic of sameness and difference that Lessing has always been obsessed by, projected now on to galactic empires, but empires still, where colonizing cultures test out their different styles of power. Her Canopeans are the ideal colonists, who rule only by virtue of their more intimate understanding of the patterns of creation and destruction at work in the universe. In fact, they rather resemble the Sufi mystics whose writings have latterly fascinated her: the point about wandering Sufi 'teachers' being that they take on the colouring of whatever culture they find themselves in, though their aim is to awaken a consciousness free of time and place. Something of their allegorizing, didactic tone has rubbed off on *Canopus in Argos* too.[29] Lessing's writing is becoming in one sense more fantastic, more fictive, and in another more urgently admonitory. In her preface to *Shikasta*, she wrote: 'Yes, I do believe that it is possible, and not only for novelists, to "plug in" to an overmind, or Ur-mind, or unconscious, or what you will'; while, two years on, the preface to *The Sirian Experiments* protests, 'No, no, I do not "believe" that there is a

82

planet called Shammat full of low-grade space pirates.' These statements show her trying, not altogether successfully, to put her fictions into a new focus. She wants them to be disposable, emblematic and analogical, so that they convey certain imaginative moves (from the personal to the collective, from the rational to the intuitive) without getting too entangled in particular histories. Readers who suspect her of believing in diabolic space pirates are responding to something that *is* there in her tone: propaganda for 'wonder', for emigration into mental space.

Perhaps she was making a private joke about her own difficulties with questions of tone and belief when she made the narrator of *The Sirian Experiments* a dry lady bureaucrat, Ambien II of the Sirian Colonial Service. The empire she serves is an enlightened technocracy riddled with existential doubt – '*who* should use *what* and *how much* and *when* and *what for?*' (*SE*, p. 81) – which treats its subject species with clinical condescension. Ambien II, an aridly correct administrator of this policy, gradually becomes troubled by the very different methods of her Canopean opposite numbers, and the novel chronicles with deliberate but dreadful slowness her millennia-long conversion to the Canopean view. The title too is a kind of slowly dawning joke: Ambien, and through her the Sirians, have all along been themselves the object of just this 'experiment' in consciousness-raising. The beginning of an answer to existential doubt is to realize that you are part of a continuous symbiotic chain, not a separate, managerial, inviolable 'I'. At the end Ambien II has learned enough to be shocked at what she sees from space of Earth's petty latterday empires:

> A grid had been stamped over the whole continent . . . a map, a chart, a certain way of thinking . . . made visible. . . . the mind of the white conquerors. Over the variety and change and differentiation of the continent, over the flows and movements and changes of the earth. (*SE*, p. 277)

It is with this image of Africa that the novel's fragile fable dissolves. And it is difficult to avoid a sensation of *déjà vu*:

83

Lessing's own mental set is showing through; *Canopus in Argos* is circling back on *Children of Violence*.

However, this return to her beginnings highlights the radical changes as well as the continuities in her imaginative life – not without attendant ironies. We note that repetition itself, for instance, is not the nightmare to her that it once was, nor is role-playing. She has settled into her alienation. Her spokesperson Ambien II, forcibly 'retired' from the Colonial Service as a subversive, reflects with sad serenity that 'It is not possible for an individual to think differently from the whole he or she is part of' (*SE*, p. 272) and that, therefore, her conventional colleagues are themselves already inwardly rejecting the official line. This may sound a pacific and consoling view, but only *in extremis*: the *un*official line, the decentred, dispersed consciousness, will triumph (though that is hardly the right way to put it) in the end, as surely as death. Indeed, in *The Making of the Representative for Planet 8*, death is another name for it, and Lessing's impatience for an ending – though it is not her final instalment – has honed down the fable into a kind of rehearsal for extinction. Planet 8, dying of cold, seems hardly to have lived; the space-fiction apparatus seems ramshackle from the start, and there is something mocking about the way she details her characters' struggle for survival – building a great wall to hold the ice, keeping up morale, waiting for the space-lift – while at the same time sowing a subversive awareness that all this 'machinery' is nonsense. What her people have to learn is mastery of mind-space: how to levitate into immortality, how to break down the wall in their psyches between matter and spirit, how to dissolve themselves into their 'alien' elements. She turns them to frost, freeze-dries them into one collective, near-anonymous voice, their 'representative'.

*

The space-odyssey format has nearly served its purpose, which was after all to bring certain things home to us. This fourth *Canopus in Argos* novel says as much, not only by the cool speed with which it dismantles its machinery, but by including, in an 'Afterword', a substantial essay about self-transcendence in a quite different context – the 1910–13 British Antarctic expedition. Scott and his men interest Lessing as specimens of a long-vanished style of heroism (and patriotism), but she is really thinking much more abstractly about changes in the 'climate' of opinion, and the mysterious laws that govern them: 'Is it possible that we could learn not to impose on each other these sacred necessities, in the name of some dogma or other. . . . Surely these are processes we can learn to study . . .?' (*MRP*, pp. 126–7).[30] Her analysis of the mental atmosphere, presaging, at the least, a new cold war, is what is wearing her fictions thin. 'No . . .', says her Planet 8 representative, 'I must not make up these tales and fabrications, comforting myself, thinking how others must be comforted' (*MRP*, p. 88).

Yet there is a shadow of comfort in rehearsing the worst, and Lessing's tone these days is oddly serene. Self-exiled in the sub-genre of speculative fiction (and rapidly using up its conventions), she has, it seems, finally confirmed her marginality. In a spirit of irony, of course, since for her it is on the margins of the culture, and of the psyche, that imaginative life survives. She has in no sense given up her claim that the writer 'represents, makes articulate . . . numbers of people who are inarticulate'. Her creature Ambien II's version – 'It is not possible for an individual to think differently from the whole he or she is part of' – is a teasing challenge from Lessing to her readers, as if to say: Alien or cold or even crazy as you may find me these days, I speak for you, especially for what you repress. Inner space has not escaped mapping, fencing and colonization, but there remain areas that will never be private property, that can only be visited in conjecture. What Lessing once wrote of Olive Schreiner strikes one as true also of herself, a measure, finally, both of her aspirations and of her displacement: that she seemed 'the sort of woman who in an older society would have been made the prophetess of a tribe.'

# NOTES

1 Doris Lessing, 'Being Prohibited', *New Statesman*, 21 April 1956; in *A Small Personal Voice*, ed. Paul Schlueter (New York: Vintage Books, 1975), pp. 157–8.

2 Doris Lessing, 'A Deep Darkness', *New Statesman*, 15 January 1971; 'African Interiors', *New Statesman*, 27 October 1961.

3 Doris Lessing, 'My Father', *Sunday Telegraph*, 1 September 1963; in *A Small Personal Voice*, pp. 89, 90, 91, 92.

4 Doris Lessing, Afterword to Olive Schreiner, *The Story of an African Farm* (New York: Fawcett World Library, 1968); in *A Small Personal Voice*, p. 108.

5 Interview with Roy Newquist, *Counterpoint* (Chicago, Ill.: Rand McNally, 1964); in *A Small Personal Voice*, pp. 45–60.

6 Ibid.

7 C. J. Driver, 'Doris Lessing: A Profile', *The New Review*, 1, 8 (November 1974), p. 20.

8 'A Conversation with Doris Lessing (1966)' (interview with Florence Howe), *Contemporary Literature*, 14, 4 (1973), p. 425.

9 Dan Jacobson, Introduction to Olive Schreiner, *The Story of an African Farm* (Harmondsworth: Penguin, 1971), p. 7.

10 Michael Thorpe, *Doris Lessing's Africa* (London: Evans, 1978), notes allusions to Conrad and (in the novel's title and one of its epigraphs) to Eliot's *The Waste Land*, but has to work hard to connect Lessing's socialist-realist reading of the colony with their more metaphysical preoccupations.

11 Ibid., p. 27.

12 Georg Lukács, *Studies in European Realism* (London: Merlin Press, 1950), p. 18.

13 Dagmar Barnouw, 'Disorderly Company: From *The Golden Notebook* to *The Four-Gated City*', *Contemporary Literature*, 14, 4 (1973), pp. 500–1.

14 Driver, op. cit., pp. 20–1.

15  All quotations from 'The Small Personal Voice' (in *Declarations*, ed. T. Maschler (London: MacGibbon & Kee, 1957)) are taken from *A Small Personal Voice*, pp. 3–21.

16  Raymond Williams, *The Long Revolution* (1961; Harmondsworth: Penguin, 1965), pp. 305, 315.

17  Philippe Sollers, *Logiques* (Paris, 1968), trans. and quoted in Jonathan Culler, *Structuralist Poetics* (1975; New York: Cornell, 1976), p. 189.

18  Hélène Cixous, 'The Character of "Character"', trans. Keith Cohen, *New Literary History*, 5, 2 (Winter 1974), p. 385.

19  Ibid., p. 388.

20  Doris Lessing, Preface to *The Golden Notebook* (Harmondsworth: Penguin, 1972); in *A Small Personal Voice*, pp. 23–43.

21  'Doris Lessing at Stony Brook: An Interview' (interview with Jonathan Raskin), *New American Review*, 8 (New York: New American Library, 1970); in *A Small Personal Voice*, p. 65.

22  Barnouw, op. cit., p. 501.

23  Ibid., p. 503.

24  Barbara Hall Rigney, *Madness and Sexual Politics in the Feminist Novel* (Madison, Wisc.: University of Wisconsin Press, 1978), pp. 77, 79.

25  'Doris Lessing at Stony Brook'; in *A Small Personal Voice*, p. 68.

26  Lynn Sukenick, 'Feeling and Reason in Doris Lessing's Fiction', *Contemporary Literature*, 14, 4 (1973), p. 530.

27  For example, Elaine Showalter in *A Literature of Their Own* (1977; London: Virago, 1978), who remains unconvinced: 'Lessing has not yet confronted the essential feminist implications of her own writing. . . . Kate Brown and the nameless "survivor" of the memoirs discard their female identities because they are unimportant in the face of impending doom. But this is not a solution; it is the equality that comes at the end of a gun' (pp. 311–13).

28  Ingrid Holmquist, in *From Society to Nature: A Study of Doris Lessing's 'Children of Violence'* (Gothenburg: Acta Universitatis Gothoburgensis, 1980), detects, with hindsight, signs of this 'ecological' concern in the earlier novels.

29  Nancy S. Hardin, 'The Sufi Teaching Story and Doris Lessing', *Twentieth Century Literature*, 23 (1977), pp. 314–26, describes some Sufi techniques for 'turning the mind round'.

30  Since I wrote this, Lessing's interest in Antarctica (and British patriotism) has become less marginal. Her performance as prophetess is in some ways impressive. However, in urging people to build shelters against the Bomb, she is (as oracles are) less than honest (see remarks on *MRP*, p. 84).

# BIBLIOGRAPHY

## WORKS BY DORIS LESSING

*Novels*

*The Grass is Singing.* London: Michael Joseph, 1950. New York: T. Y. Crowell, 1950.

*Children of Violence*
*Martha Quest.* London: Michael Joseph, 1952. New York: Simon & Schuster, 1964.
*A Proper Marriage.* London: Michael Joseph, 1954. New York: Simon & Schuster, 1964.
*A Ripple from the Storm.* London: Michael Joseph, 1958. New York: Simon & Schuster, 1966.
*Landlocked.* London: MacGibbon & Kee, 1965. New York: Simon & Schuster, 1966.
*The Four-Gated City.* London: MacGibbon & Kee, 1969. New York: Knopf, 1969.

*Retreat to Innocence.* London: Michael Joseph, 1956.
*The Golden Notebook.* London: Michael Joseph, 1962. New York: Simon & Schuster, 1962.
*Briefing for a Descent into Hell.* London: Cape, 1971. New York: Knopf, 1971.
*The Summer Before the Dark.* London: Cape, 1973. New York: Knopf, 1973.
*The Memoirs of a Survivor.* London: Octagon Press, 1974. New York: Knopf, 1975.

*Canopus in Argos: Archives*
*Re: Colonized Planet 5, Shikasta.* London: Cape, 1979. New York: Knopf, 1979.
*The Marriages Between Zones Three, Four, and Five.* London: Cape, 1980. New York: Knopf, 1980.

*The Sirian Experiments.* London: Cape, 1981. New York: Knopf, 1981.

*The Making of the Representative for Planet 8.* London: Cape, 1982. New York: Knopf, 1982.

## Shorter fiction

*This Was the Old Chief's Country.* London: Michael Joseph, 1951. New York: T. Y. Crowell, 1952.

*Five.* London: Michael Joseph, 1953.

*The Habit of Loving.* London: MacGibbon & Kee, 1957. New York: T. Y. Crowell, 1957.

*A Man and Two Women.* London: MacGibbon & Kee, 1963. New York: Simon & Schuster, 1963.

*African Stories.* London: Michael Joseph, 1964. New York: Simon & Schuster, 1965.

*The Story of a Non-Marrying Man and Other Stories.* London: Cape, 1972. Published as *The Temptation of Jack Orkeney and Other Stories,* New York: Knopf, 1972.

*This Was the Old Chief's Country. Collected African Stories,* Vol. 1. London: Michael Joseph, 1973.

*The Sun Between Their Feet. Collected African Stories,* Vol. 2. London: Michael Joseph, 1973.

*To Room Nineteen. Collected Stories,* Vol. 1. London: Cape, 1978.

*The Temptation of Jack Orkeney. Collected Stories,* Vol. 2. London: Cape, 1978.

## Plays

*Each His Own Wilderness.* In *New English Dramatists: Three Plays,* ed. E. Martin Browne. Harmondsworth: Penguin, 1959.

*Play with a Tiger.* London: Michael Joseph, 1962.

## Non-fiction

*Going Home.* With drawings by Paul Hogarth. London: Michael Joseph, 1957. Rev. edn, London: Panther, 1968. New York: Ballantine, 1968.

*In Pursuit of the English: A Documentary.* London: MacGibbon & Kee, 1960. New York: Simon & Schuster, 1961.

*Particularly Cats.* London: Michael Joseph, 1967. New York: Simon & Schuster, 1967.

## Selected articles, essays and interviews

'Myself as Sportsman'. *New Yorker,* 21 (21 January 1956), pp. 78–82.

'Being Prohibited'. *New Statesman*, 21 April 1956, pp. 410–12. Repr. in *A Small Personal Voice*, pp. 155–60.

'The Small Personal Voice'. In *Declaration*, ed. T. Maschler, pp. 12–27. London: MacGibbon & Kee, 1957. Repr. in *A Small Personal Voice*, pp. 3–21.

'My Father'. *Sunday Telegraph*, 1 September 1963. Repr. in *A Small Personal Voice*, pp. 83–93.

Interview with Roy Newquist. In *Counterpoint*, pp. 414–24. Chicago, Ill.: Rand McNally, 1964. Repr. in *A Small Personal Voice*, pp. 45–60.

'Afterword'. Olive Schreiner, *The Story of an African Farm*, pp. 273–90. New York: Fawcett World Library, 1968. Repr. in *A Small Personal Voice*, pp. 97–120.

'A Conversation with Doris Lessing (1966)'. Interview with Florence Howe. *Contemporary Literature*, 14, 4 (1973), pp. 418–36.

'Doris Lessing at Stony Brook: An Interview'. Interview with Jonathan Raskin. *New American Review*, 8, pp. 166–79. New York: New American Library, 1970. Repr. in *A Small Personal Voice*, pp. 61–82.

'In the World, Not of It'. *Encounter*, 39, 2 (August 1972).

*A Small Personal Voice: Essays, Reviews, Interviews*. Ed. Paul Schlueter. New York: Knopf, 1974.

'The Ones Who Know'. *The Times Literary Supplement*, 30 April 1976, pp. 514–15.


# BIBLIOGRAPHY

Burkom, Selina R. 'A Doris Lessing Checklist'. *Critique*, 2, 1 (1969), pp. 69–81.

Ipp, Catharina. *Doris Lessing: A Bibliography*. Johannesburg: University of Witwatersrand, 1967.

Krouse, Agate Nesante. 'A Doris Lessing Checklist'. *Contemporary Literature*, 14, 4 (1973), pp. 590–7.

See also the *Doris Lessing Newsletter*, published by the Doris Lessing Society (English Department, Old Dominion University, Norfolk, Virginia).

# SELECTED CRITICISM OF DORIS LESSING

*Books*

Brewster, Dorothy. *Doris Lessing*. New York: Twayne, 1965.

Holmquist, Ingrid. *From Society to Nature: A Study of Doris Lessing's 'Children of Violence'*. Gothenburg: Acta Universitatis Gothoburgensis, 1980.

Pratt, A., and Dembo, L. S. (eds). *Doris Lessing: Critical Studies*. Madison, Wisc.: University of Wisconsin Press, 1974.

Rigney, Barbara Hall. *Madness and Sexual Politics in the Feminist Novel*. Madison, Wisc.: University of Wisconsin Press, 1978.

Rubenstein, Roberta. *The Novelistic Vision of Doris Lessing: Breaking the Forms of Consciousness*. Urbana and Chicago, Ill., and London: University of Illinois Press, 1979.

Schlueter, Paul. *The Novels of Doris Lessing*. Carbondale, Ill.: Southern Illinois University Press, 1973.

Singleton, Mary Ann. *The City and the Veld: The Fiction of Doris Lessing*. London: Associated University Presses, 1977.

Thorpe, Michael. *Doris Lessing's Africa*. London: Evans, 1978.


*Selected articles*

Barnouw, Dagmar. 'Disorderly Company: From *The Golden Notebook* to *The Four-Gated City*'. *Contemporary Literature*, 14 (1973), pp. 491–514.

Drabble, Margaret. 'Doris Lessing: Cassandra in a World Under Siege'. *Ramparts*, 10 (1972), pp. 50–4.

Driver, C. J. 'Doris Lessing: A Profile'. *The New Review*, 1, 8 (1974), pp. 17–23.

Hardin, Nancy S. 'The Sufi Teaching Story and Doris Lessing'. *Twentieth Century Literature*, 23 (1977), pp. 314–26.

Karl, Frederick R. 'Doris Lessing in the Sixties: The New Anatomy of Melancholy'. *Contemporary Literature*, 13 (1972), pp. 15–33.

Morgan, Ellen. 'Alienation of the Woman Writer in *The Golden Notebook*'. *Contemporary Literature*, 14 (1973), pp. 471–80.

Spilka, Mark. 'Lessing and Lawrence: The Battle of the Sexes'. *Contemporary Literature*, 15 (1975), pp. 218–40.

Sukenick, Lynn. 'Feeling and Reason in Doris Lessing's Fiction'. *Contemporary Literature*, 14 (1973), pp. 515–35.

Vlastos, Marion. 'Doris Lessing and R. D. Laing: Psychopolitics and Prophecy'. *PMLA*, 91 (1976), pp. 245–58.